Praise for the Australian Edition

'It's a long time since I have read a radical book like *Growth Fetish*.
I had forgotten how energisin  *Age*

'An incisive critique of hov   tical
systems have turned us int   you
choose to do and wherever yo   ng a
copy of *Growth Fetish* tucked ι   hor
of *The Future Eaters*

'A call to arms for the *No Logo* generation.' – Simon Noble,
Australian Review of Political Economy

'*Growth Fetish* ... became a best-seller in Australia, a very unusual
feat for what is normally considered a very dry subject. The book
has been the subject of much controversy, and has managed to
infuriate commentators on both the left and right of the politico-
economic debate.' – Wikipedia

'Australia's most amazing economist... you will find [*Growth Fetish*]
either exhilarating or deeply threatening.' – Ross Gittens,
Economics Editor, *Sydney Morning Herald*

'This book reveals the undelivered reality of economic growth and
the hollow mantras of the Third Way. *Growth Fetish* provides a
much needed road map to a new politics in a post-growth world.' –
Australian Senator Natasha Stott Despoja

'Clive Hamilton's work is just silly, dangerous, left-wing crap.' –
Michael Egan, Labor State Treasurer, New South Wales

'The most lucid, penetrating, comprehensive and clearly articulated
analysis of our present human predicament and of the pathologies
that underlie it that I've seen so far.' – John Bunzl, author of *The
Simultaneous Policy*

'*Growth Fetish* argues that advanced economies, obsessed with
increasing gross domestic product, should chill out.' – David Smith,
Economics Editor, *Sunday Times*

'Breaks new ground ... Clearly, stylishly written.' – Professor Hugh
Stretton, author of *Economics: A New Introduction*

'A broadside against the underlying values of contemporary
consumer capitalism – bound to trigger major controversy...' –
Professor Frank Stilwell, *Journal of Australian Political Economy*

Hilary Wardhaugh

Clive Hamilton is Executive Director of The Australia Institute, Australia's foremost public interest think tank. Trained in economics and politics, he also holds academic positions at the Australian National University and the University of Technology Sydney.

GROWTH FETISH

Clive Hamilton

Pluto  Press

LONDON • STERLING, VIRGINIA

First published 2003 by Allen & Unwin, Australia

This edition published 2004 by Pluto Press
345 Archway Road, London N6 5AA
and 22883 Quicksilver Drive, Sterling, VA 20166–2012, USA

www.plutobooks.com

British Library Cataloguing in Publication Data
A catalogue record for this book is available from the British Library

ISBN   0 7453 2251 4 hardback
ISBN   0 7453 2250 6 paperback

Library of Congress Cataloging in Publication Data applied for

10   9   8   7   6   5   4   3   2   1

Typeset in Australia by Bookhouse, Sydney
Printed and bound in the European Union by
MPG Books, Bodmin, England

All great truths begin as blasphemies.
George Bernard Shaw

I am indebted to Hugh Stretton, Noam Chomsky and Frank Stilwell for suggesting improvements to the manuscript and providing encouragement. My understanding of the post-modern world has been deepened by Myra Hamilton. Chris Pirie has been an excellent editor. The support of the Australia Institute and the Poola Foundation have made preparation of this book possible, and the Graduate Program in Public Policy at the Australian National University has provided a quiet and supportive environment for writing. I am also grateful to Elizabeth Weiss of Allen & Unwin for her faith in the project.

Contents

Introduction

For two decades, under the withering force of free market ideology, the Left has been wandering in the wilderness. It continues to declaim while no one listens, mouthing the old slogans to a world that no longer cares. After the fall of the Berlin Wall and the final 'discrediting' of socialism, the Left had nowhere to turn and the vacuum was filled by the politics of the Third Way, represented most evidently by the policies and style of Tony Blair in Britain. For many, the Third Way has been a pallid, even apologetic, response to the depredations of neoliberalism—little more than Thatcherism with a human face.

Just as there has been no coherent rebuttal of neoliberalism, there has been no lucid critique of the ideas of the Third Way, despite widespread discomfort with it as a political program. This is no accident: the Third Way shares its most fundamental beliefs with the neoliberalism of the First Way, the beliefs that the central objective of government must be the promotion of economic growth and that markets must prevail. Like their conservative counterparts, Third Way politicians argue that the answer to almost every problem is more economic growth. The Third Way is a victim of the great contradiction of the modern world—that, despite several decades of sustained economic growth, our societies are no happier than they were. Growth not only fails to make people contented; it destroys many of the things that do. Growth fosters empty consumerism, degrades the natural environment, weakens social cohesion and corrodes character. Yet we are told, ad nauseam, that there is no alternative.

The politics of the Third Way feels inauthentic, and its practitioners are often criticised for putting style before substance. It deals awkwardly with post-industrial social movements. In particular, the challenges posed by the environment and women's movements are treated as little more than new items to be added to the political program—items that move up and down the agenda according to the opinion polls. Third Way politics thus marginalises what are seen by many as the most compelling reasons for radical social change.

The leadership of the Left is responsible for this state of affairs. In a social structure that has been thoroughly transformed by five post-war decades of consumer capitalism, it has failed miserably to develop the new ideas that would promote a more just and sustainable community. Difficult as it might be to admit, social democrats and democratic socialists have a predisposition to believe that the mass of people are suffering from material deprivation. The Left thrives on the imagined wretchedness of others. When the economy goes bad the Left feels vindicated: the reason to condemn the system is renewed. The Left revels in a sort of collective Schadenfreude.

But in the West today the Left's 'deprivation model' is the opposite of the truth. The dominant characteristic of contemporary society is not deprivation but abundance. By any standard, the countries of Western Europe and North America, plus Japan and Australasia, are enormously wealthy. Most of their citizens want for nothing. Average real incomes have risen at least three-fold since the end of the Second World War. Most people are prosperous beyond the dreams of their parents and grandparents. The houses of typical families are bigger than ever and are filled with big-screen TVs and DVDs and racks of unused clothes. They are centrally heated and air-conditioned; many have swimming pools or pool tables; most have unused rooms; expensive cars are parked outside. It is nothing for an average parent to spend several hundred dollars on a present for a child or to buy them a personal mobile phone. Citizens have access to sophisticated health care when they need it, and almost everyone has access to good-quality primary and secondary education. Despite the availability of free education, large numbers of households with no more than average incomes choose to outlay tens of thousands of dollars to send their children to private schools and then to universities.

In a world characterised by abundance rather than deprivation, the Left is preoccupied with the distribution of income, insistent that capitalism always leads to greater inequality. This is patently untrue. Since the Second World War the distribution of income has at times become more equal and at times less equal, and when it has been deteriorating in some countries it has been improving in others. But the fact is that the great majority who once lived in material deprivation no longer do. Of course, there is a residue at the bottom who continue to struggle; we still have poverty, something sustained growth and protracted efforts have failed to eliminate. As a society we have an obligation to attempt ceaselessly to eradicate poverty, but why does the Left continue to base its entire political philosophy and strategy on the circumstances of the bottom ten per cent? This is a philosophy that has more in common with the ethic of Christian charity than of radical social change.

Concern for the underprivileged—however well founded it might be—should not provide the driving force for a politics of social change in a society where the daily life of the great majority is occupied with how best to dispose of their wealth. Yet the world view of the Left is predicated on a model of society in which the dominant social evil is want. Rooted historically in the mass deprivation of the inter-war years, the preoccupation with material living standards has been rendered irrelevant by five decades of economic growth. The social model of the Left is dramatically outdated and completely at odds with the real circumstances of the great majority of ordinary people.

But what of the poor in the developing countries of the South? Surely they need more growth? Yes, they do, as long as it is growth of the right sort and not the type that feeds the extravagant lifestyles of crony capitalists and the power of rapacious finance houses. But the modern Left has become much too preoccupied with North–South questions. In railing against globalisation and the pernicious influence of multinational corporations, it has effectively abandoned hope of social change at home and vacated domestic political space, allowing it to be occupied by the Right. While 'anti-globalisation' protests can be inspirational and can even succeed in slowing down the processes of international economic integration, the protesters have no coherent strategy for political change; in fact, they have no agreed objectives. What does the anti-globalisation Left want? Consumer capitalism and the powers that are sustained by it will never be transformed internationally unless they are assailed first at home. The Left must come home.

Over the last three decades two narratives have been heard within the Left. The first is the traditional 'deprivation model', in which the world is understood as a place where people are struggling to make ends meet, where there is a widening gap between rich and poor, where a huge underclass is being excluded from the rewards of globalisation, and where the labour market is a place of insecurity, entrenched unemployment and increasing exploitation. In this discourse, the central conflict remains that between labour and capital in the sphere of production, and the appropriate organisational response is trade unionism.

The second narrative describes a world where waste and over-consumption are rife, where growth and development are out of control, where materialism and consumerism are driving out the values of community, and where pervasive marketing deludes the masses. In this discourse, the central conflict is between the cultural and political influence of corporations and the demand for genuine democracy, personal autonomy, and protection of natural and cultural values; the appropriate organisational response takes the form of new social movements that challenge the political and cultural influence of the corporate world.

Both discourses occur on the left, but at best they are discordant and at worst incompatible. One stresses material deprivation; the other emphasises the excesses of growth and consumption. Failure to reconcile the two has meant political turmoil, manifested in increasingly desperate attempts by modern social democratic parties to hold on to their old working-class constituencies while appealing to the newer middle-class progressive constituencies that have evolved out of feminism, environmentalism and concern for human rights and global justice. In these attempts, they are failing both groups.

This book argues for a different understanding of the discontents of modern society and proposes an alternative political program, one that I call 'eudemonism' (pronounced with the emphasis on the long *e* in the second syllable). The new, post-growth political philosophy of eudemonism proposes a society in which people can pursue the activities that truly can improve their individual and collective wellbeing. It is built on a consideration of the evidence for what does and does not contribute to a more contented society. The extensive empirical as well as philosophical literature on this subject confirms commonsense perceptions that are widely held but rarely acted upon.

Eudemonism provides an alternative to neoliberalism, the Third Way, and the deprivation model of the traditional Left. It is well understood why an alternative to unbridled neoliberalism is needed, but the urgent task is to go beyond the traditional preoccupations of social democracy without abandoning the commitment to justice and liberation. The deprivation model saps progressive people of their creative energy, not only because they are co-opted into supporting the fundamental goal of neoliberalism but also, and crucially, because it prevents the Left from joining with what is perhaps the most serious political and intellectual challenge to consumer capitalism—environmentalism. The new perspective resolves the dissonance between the Left's preoccupation with deprivation and environmentalists' emphasis on the perils of abundance. Put starkly, one wants more growth and one wants less.

Adherence to the deprivation model explains why social democratic and labour parties find it so difficult to truly separate themselves from their conservative opponents. Even if one believes that economic growth is maximised by putting some constraints on the operation of markets, one can still do no other than appeal to the self-centred individualism of the marketing society, of people who attempt to give meaning to their lives through their consumption behaviour. Moreover, growth fetishism cedes enormous power to the claims of business: a social democracy that does not strike fear in the boardrooms is no social democracy at all.

The political implications of all of this are profound. It must be accepted that capitalism has moved to a phase of abundance, and abundance broadly spread. Eudemonism requires us to focus on the things that really do affect the wellbeing of ordinary people and the processes that condition society. Yet despite its fantastic material progress, and at a time of complete political dominance, capitalism has never been more fragile. Why? With more wealth at their disposal than ever before, most people could simply choose not to participate—to step off the materialist treadmill, to ignore the advertisements, to eschew the latest electronic gadget, the second house, the luxury car, the holidays abroad, the meaningless acquisitions. To do so would not require them to take to the barricades or put themselves on the breadline. All it takes is an open recognition that personal contentment is more important than money. But change in the political structure is needed to facilitate the transition, a strategy I call 'political down-shifting'.

Today, the compulsion to participate in the consumer society is not prompted by material need or by political coercion: it is prompted by the belief of the great mass of ordinary people that to find happiness they must be richer, regardless of how wealthy they already are. If ordinary people today are exploited, it is by common consent. Responding to the lures of the marketers, they choose the gilded cage and would prefer not to be told that the door is open. We need a politics that points out that the door is open—not just for the rich but for ordinary people too—a politics that allows people to achieve liberation, to find authenticity, and to value community and relationships above wealth and status. In short, now that the economic problem has been solved we need a politics that encourages people to pursue a rich life instead of a life of riches.

This book presents a critique of consumer capitalism and outlines the ideas and structures for a post-growth society. The politics of the transition to a post-growth society does not call for the overthrow of the state or the destruction of capital; it starts from where we are. Yet the society described here represents a radical rejection of the ideology and social structures of growth fetishism. If history has ended then it must be restarted, for the post-growth society is the stage of history beyond global consumer capitalism. The new politics of happiness will transform power structures, our attitudes to the natural world and the way we think about our lives and our relationships. Such a politics would rob the market of its most powerful weapon, people's willingness to transform themselves into consumers. A post-growth politics would deprive capital of much of its political power, because people everywhere would reject the assumption that everything—including our communities, the natural world and our dignity—should be sacrificed on the altar of growth.

Most people on the left scoffed when Frances Fukuyama announced that the triumph of liberal capitalism meant the 'end of history'. But apart from descent into techno-barbarism, what is to succeed it?

Growth fetishism

The growth fetish

Nothing more preoccupies the modern political process than economic growth. As never before, it is the touchstone of policy success. Countries rate their progress against others by their income per person, which can rise only through faster growth. High growth is a cause of national pride; low growth attracts accusations of incompetence in the case of rich countries and pity in the case of poor countries. A country that experiences a period of low growth goes through an agony of national soul-searching, in which pundits of the left and right expostulate about 'where we went wrong' and whether there is some fault in the national character.

Every newspaper, every day, quotes a political leader or a commentator arguing that we need more economic growth to improve national wellbeing and build a better society. The release of the quarterly national accounts unfailingly receives extensive coverage. Picking out growth in gross national product (GNP), journalists write as if they have an infallible technical barometer of a nation's progress. Derived by some of the best statisticians using the internationally agreed system of national accounting, GNP appears to provide a measure of prosperity that is immune to argument. If GNP growth reaches or exceeds expectations, government leaders crow about their achievements. If it falls below expectations, opposition parties attack the government for its ineptitude. Throughout history national leaders have promised freedom, equality, mass education, moral invigoration and the restoration of national pride; now they promise more economic growth.

In the thrall of the growth fetish, all the major political parties in the West have made themselves captives of the national accounts. The parties may differ on social policy, but there is unchallengeable consensus that the overriding objective of government must be growth of the economy. The parties fighting elections each promise to manage the economy better, so that economic growth will be higher. The answer to almost every problem is 'more economic growth'. Unemployment is rife: only growth can create the jobs. Schools and hospitals are under-funded: growth will improve the budget. Protection of the environment is unaffordable: the solution is growth. Poverty is entrenched: growth will rescue the poor. Income distribution is unequal: growth will make everyone better off. For decades we have been promised that growth will unlock possibilities that previous generations could only dream about. Economic growth will deliver a life of ever-increasing leisure, more free services, devices to relieve the drudgery of household work, opportunities for personal enrichment, exciting space travel, and cures for the diseases of humankind. The lure of growth is endless.

But, in the face of the fabulous promises of economic growth, at the beginning of the 21st century we are confronted by an awful fact. Despite high and sustained levels of economic growth in the West over a period of 50 years—growth that has seen average real incomes increase several times over—the mass of people are no more satisfied with their lives now than they were then. If growth is intended to give us better lives, and there can be no other purpose, it has failed. This fact is proved in Chapter 2 but in the meantime the reader can simply ask this question: Do I believe that on the whole people are happier now than they were 40 or 50 years ago? When asked this, almost everyone says 'no'.

The more we examine the role of growth in modern society, the more our obsession with growth appears to be a fetish—that is, an inanimate object worshipped for its apparent magical powers. Economic growth purports to be a very ordinary idea, no more than an increase in the volume of goods and services produced each year. But closer analysis reveals that it 'abounds in metaphysical subtleties and theological niceties'.[1] The product of growth, which for ordinary people takes the form of its universal equivalent, money income, represents of course much more than a greater ability to consume. Increase in income is the very object of life in modern society, in which all the hopes and schemes of men and women are invested. Indeed, as is argued in Chapter 3, increasing income has become pivotal to the creation and reproduction of self in modern society. Thus growth takes on significance not because it multiplies the pile of goods and services available for consumption but because of the excitation it produces in people, the promise of bliss it holds.

In the 1930s and 1940s Papua New Guinea witnessed a proliferation of religious movements predicting an imminent new age of plenty. The people believed that the new age would be initiated by the arrival of 'cargo' sent by supernatural beings—a belief that grew from observing planes and ships that arrived from nowhere and brought cargo to colonial officials. Sometimes members of cargo cults built symbolic landing strips and warehouses, in preparation for the arrival of cargo, and abandoned traditional sources of sustenance as a mundane distraction.

Westerners might mock cargo cults as primitive superstition, but there are strong parallels with the modern growth fetish. Cargo cults and the growth fetish both invest magical powers in the properties of material goods, possession of which is believed to provide for a paradise on earth. This state can be attained through more cargo or more money; each has prophets whose role is to persuade ordinary people to keep the faith, to believe that more cargo or more money will arrive and will take believers to a plane of ecstasy. While the colonialists who ruled over the cult members were defined by their possession of large amounts of cargo, those who rule over people in the grip of the growth fetish are defined by their ownership of large amounts of money, and in both groups there is a widespread belief that anyone can join the elite by acquiring similar magnitudes of cargo or money. Westerners seem to differ in that they understand that the cargo does not appear from nowhere but must be produced, although many people believe that fortunes can be conjured from thin air, through pyramid selling, lotteries, stock market speculation, tax evasion, or myriads of get-rich-quick schemes. Even those who do no more than write books on get-rich-quick schemes often get rich quickly. Like the cargo cultists, many Westerners are willing to abandon more traditional forms of sustenance, such as a nine-to-five job, in order to pursue manna.

Growth fetishism is not confined to advanced countries. Developing countries are also obsessed—perhaps the last and most potent legacy of colonialism. They have little choice. Were they to deviate from the pursuit of maximum economic growth, we can be sure that, if 'the markets' did not exact retribution, the IMF and the World Bank would. The 'Asian miracle' was a miracle of growth. Determined to beat the West at its own game, the little tigers learned to roar by sustaining growth rates of 8 per cent, 9 per cent and even 10 per cent a year over a decade or two. In one of history's great reversals, Western commentators and market pundits in the 1980s began to berate their own governments for failing to match the growth performance of East Asia: the strategies of the little tigers became the model to be emulated. This usually meant faster trade liberalisation, lower wages, labour market 'flexibility', and deep cuts in taxation and social security. The tigers of East Asia had apparently learnt their lessons from the industrialised countries so well that they had become the teachers, and political leaders in the West became the dutiful students. Why? Because 8 per cent is higher than 4 per cent.

The East Asian tigers drew their inspiration from Japan, seen the world over as a voracious growth machine. We will consider later the malaise into which the Japanese economy sank in the

1990s, but for now it is worth quoting one of the most astute observers of that country, Gavan McCormack:

> The goal of attaining something like Japanese consumption levels has driven growth in much of Asia since at least the Vietnam War, and has come to define the kind of future to which people aspire. Japan is thought to have found, deciphered, and put into practice an alchemical formula for growth and prosperity. It constitutes both model and magnet, pulling upon the entire Asian region . . . In no country is social life so structured around the imperatives of economic life, or are people subjected to more pressure to consume. Nowhere is the emptiness of affluence more deeply felt.[2]

Socialist countries too were smitten by growth. The Cold War ideological divide was not about the desirability of economic growth. On that all agreed. What they disagreed about was which system of economic organisation—socialism or capitalism—could generate more growth. 'Scientific socialists' set out to prove that a properly planned and managed economy based on collective ownership of the means of production could surpass capitalism in improving the standard of living of ordinary people. It could do so because the people would be working for themselves, rather than being exploited, and because a socialist system could avoid the crippling economic crises that were integral to capitalism. The early successes of the Soviet space program shocked the United States: they seemed to suggest that the socialist system had superior productive power.

Although Karl Marx had devoted much of his early writing to the psychological impact of wage labour under capitalism—how proletarians became alienated from their true nature, and the liberating effect of free men and women working collectively for the common good—in practice socialism in Eastern Europe quickly became preoccupied with industrial production. Lenin adopted the slogan 'Soviets plus electrification'. In China it took longer: the struggle to create new socialist men and women raged through the '50s, '60s and '70s, until the pragmatic leadership of Deng Zhao Ping turned China onto the capitalist road and an orgy of money making. Growth fetishism now grips China. It has been hailed by the apologists of growth in the West, but many, within China and without, are now asking: Is this what the great Chinese experiment with socialism has come to?

Economists on wellbeing

There can be little doubt that in recent decades the most evangelical promoters of growth fetishism have been the economists, whose profession has since the 1970s dominated public debate and policy formation throughout the world. Economists—or, at least, that part of the profession that has had most influence since the early 1980s—are relentless advocates of more growth as the solution to all problems, and as a profession have become wholly uncritical of the economic system. One particular school of economists has achieved uncontested control: the neoclassical or free-market school. Even before the neoclassical school won the day, the rival schools of Keynesians, Ricardians and Marxists largely accepted the pre-eminence of growth, albeit with an equal emphasis on the distribution of the fruits of growth. Only the Institutionalist school, associated with names such as Veblen and Galbraith, seriously questioned the goals of the system by pointing out the corrosive effects of 'conspicuous consumption', consumer emptiness and 'private affluence, public squalor'.

Today, the benefits of growth are taken to be so self-evident that one has to search hard to find any reference to them in economics texts. Open any university text and the subject is immediately defined as the study of how to use scarce resources to best satisfy unlimited wants. These 'wants' are assumed to be those that consumption satisfies, and the first half of the text is occupied with analysis of the behaviour of consumers in their quest to maximise their 'utility'. By subtle fusion, human beings have become 'consumers' and human desire has been defined in terms of goods; it follows that the only way to make people happier is to provide more goods. In other words, the objective is growth. The other half of the textbook is devoted to macro-economics, a subject whose purpose is above all to understand how the government should manage the economy so that the growth rate is maximised over time.

Economists have not always been uncritical advocates of growth. The early economists understood that their task was to explore the human condition and the progress of nations. This was, of course, the case with moral philosopher and political economist Adam Smith, whose analysis of how markets work has been so bastardised by 20th century advocates of free markets. The neoliberal Right's cannibalisation of Smith's work is a historical libel. Writing in 1865, John Stuart Mill devoted sustained attention to a concept that would be unthinkable to today's economists and policy makers—the idea of the stationary state. Like many of his contemporaries, he believed that any serious discussion of the relationship between economic growth and human wellbeing leads ineluctably to a consideration of the stationary state. Mill asked, 'Towards what ultimate point is society tending by its industrial progress? When the progress ceases, in what condition are we to expect that it will leave mankind?'[3] One searches in vain for any mention of these questions in modern economics texts. In a passage whose sentiments have a surprisingly modern ring, Mill declared that he had no aversion to a stationary state of capital and wealth:

> I confess I am not charmed with the ideal of life held out by those who think that the normal state of human beings is that of struggling to get on; that the trampling, crushing, elbowing, and treading on each other's heels, which form the existing type of social life, are the most desirable lot of human kind, or anything but the disagreeable symptoms of one of the phases of industrial progress . . . the best state for human nature is that in which, while no one is poor, no one desires to be richer, nor has any reason to fear being thrust back by the efforts of others to push themselves forward.[4]

There have been few dissenters in recent times, but one of the most penetrating was E.J. Mishan. In a prescient essay published in 1967, Mishan, then Reader in Economics at the London School of Economics, prefigured some of the most powerful critiques of growth to come from outside the profession. He prefaced his essay with the observation that popular post-war political debates served only to confuse the chief question that confronted Britain: whether to seek to adjust the environment to gratify human nature or to adjust human nature to preserve the environment. Mishan's book, *The Costs of Economic Growth*, exposed the mystical reverence in which GNP growth had come to be held: 'Apparently one has but to consult it to comprehend the entire condition of society. Among the faithful . . . any doubt that, say, a four per cent growth rate . . . is better for the nation than a three per cent growth rate is near-heresy; is tantamount to a doubt that four is greater than three'.[5]

While doubters such as Mishan could still find a publisher in the 1960s, the economic and political changes of the 1970s put an end to that. The history of the world entered a new phase. Confronted by simultaneous inflation and unemployment in the emerging globalised world, Keynesianism was forced onto the back foot. At the same time, right-wing intellectual activists began lifting the nostrums of neoclassical economics from the textbooks and turning them into policy prescriptions. This task was left in large part to right-wing think tanks outside academe. The canon of neoliberalism that emerged swept away the Left and has faced no serious intellectual or political challenge.

The fact that neoliberalism remains unchallenged is extraordinary given the events of recent history, for laissez-faire capitalism has been marked by devastating failures. The transition of Eastern Europe from central planning to private ownership and free markets has plunged citizens of those countries into material poverty and social chaos, creating a new form of criminal capitalism. World markets have become extraordi-

narily volatile and are now dominated by exchange rate specula-
tors, so that various countries, often for no good reason, have
been thrown into crisis by speculative attacks on their currencies, resulting in widespread and prolonged misery. In addition,
the costs of economic growth, which fall largely outside the
marketplace and so do not appear in the national accounts, have
become inescapably apparent—in the form of disturbing signs
of ecological decline, an array of social problems that growth has
failed to correct, and epidemics of unemployment, overwork and
insecurity. Finally (and this a theme to which I return repeatedly), despite succeeding in delivering much higher incomes for
the majority of people, those societies are characterised by a
prevading and deep-rooted malaise. The neoliberal growth
project has failed. The dismal science has a dismal record.

After sustained attacks from outside the profession, a few
economists have at last acknowledged that the link between
growth and wellbeing may not be self-evident. But no serious
consideration is given to the critique; after all, conceding that
more economic growth may not make people any better off would
be a fatal blow to economists—attacking their credibility, their
influence, and their jealously guarded place as conjurors of cargo.
Gregory Mankiw, regarded as one of the more enlightened economists of the 1990s and author of an influential US textbook, is
typical in devoting two pages in a volume of nearly 800 to the
question of the relationship between GDP and wellbeing. But,
rather than take up the serious arguments or consider the moun-
tain of empirical evidence, Mankiw resorts to platitudes and
tautologies in defence of GDP: 'Because most people would prefer
to receive higher income and enjoy higher expenditure, GDP per

person seems a natural measure of the economic well-being of the average individual'.[6] As we will see, the idea that it makes sense to measure a person's wellbeing by the amount of money they have is in fact highly contentious. But what may slip by in Mankiw's apparently innocuous statement is the reliance of neoliberal economists on the belief that what people as individuals *prefer* is, always and everywhere, good for them. An alcoholic would prefer more drinks, but we don't measure their wellbeing by the number of drinks they have.

The economists have a well-worn escape route: 'We have nothing to say about how people's preferences are formed. We are not psychologists or sociologists, we just take preferences as given'. On this the elaborate structure of economics is built. More importantly, it provides the ideological basis for neoliberal philosophy and free-market policies. But what the economists, philosophers and policy makers do not want pointed out is that the markets themselves influence preferences. If consumers do not act in their own interests or can serve their interests only by acting collectively (subjects I return to), the whole structure of neoliberalism begins to crumble.

For the most part, neoliberal economists are schooled in mathematics and economic theory and are innocent of philosophy, psychology and history. They are notorious for their ignorance of the fact that neoclassical economics embodies a specific philosophical position known as 'utilitarianism'. So, for them, just as the capitalist firm described in the textbooks transforms inputs into goods and services for the market, wellbeing is produced by pouring goods and services into a receptacle marked 'human being'—as if people were production processes that convert commodities into happiness. Thus Mankiw, forced to concede that GDP does not directly measure those things that make life worthwhile, declares nevertheless that 'it does measure our ability to obtain the inputs into a worthwhile life'.[7]

Neoliberal economists have simply grown up absorbing the ideology of growth and are now, like Soviet apparatchiks, unable to question it. Some of their eminent predecessors were more sensitive to the questions of wellbeing and economics. Even the originators of the system of national accounts that now rules our lives were acutely conscious of its limitations. John Maynard Keynes, John Hicks and Simon Kuznets first developed the system of national accounting because their governments needed better ways of managing their economies in the face of dramatic swings in the business cycle between the world wars. These economists repeatedly warned against using measures such as GNP as indicators of prosperity. Kuznets, the originator of the system of uniform national accounts in the United States, warned Congress in 1934, 'The welfare of a nation can scarcely be inferred from a measurement of national income . . .'[8] Kuznets watched in dismay as his warnings were ignored and economists and policy makers grew accustomed to equating prosperity with growth in national income. By 1962 he was writing that the construction and use of the system of national accounting must be rethought: 'Distinctions must be kept in mind between quantity and quality of growth, between its costs and returns, and between the short and the long run . . . Goals for 'more' growth should specify more growth of what and for what'.[9] The warnings went unheeded.

The great contradiction

In 1995 a report prepared for the Merck Family Fund launched a devastating attack on growth fetishism in the United States. *Yearning for Balance* reports the results of a detailed investigation, through a national survey and focus groups, of US citizens' perspectives on consumption and the American lifestyle.[10] The report reached four important conclusions. First, Americans believe that the value system that dominates their society is wrong: 'They believe materialism, greed, and selfishness increasingly dominate American life, crowding out a more meaningful set of values centered on family, responsibility, and community'.[11] The vast majority want their lives to be based on values of family closeness, friendship, and individual and social responsibility, yet they believe their society fails to promote these values. They desperately want to achieve a balance between the material and non-material sides of their lives, since the latter has been driven out by greed.

Second, Americans believe that materialism has overtaken society, with dire consequences; that 'lust' for material things lies at the root of crime, family breakdown and drug addiction. Four-fifths believe they consume far more than they need to and are concerned about the inability of people today to save for the things they want. Children are considered to be especially possessed by a corrupting materialism. Third, Americans are ambivalent about the contradiction they face. They can see that materialism is corroding society and themselves, but they are too fearful to change their behaviour in any significant way. They are wedded to 'financial security', even though they understand that non-material aspirations are the ones that will give them contented lives. They therefore avoid too close an examination of their own behaviour, yet the contradiction gives rise to a deep conflict of conscience.

Finally, Americans understand, albeit somewhat vaguely, that rampant consumerism is destroying the natural environment. There is an overwhelming concern that the world left for their children will be less safe and less secure and will have the wrong value system. In stark contrast with the optimism of the post-war boom, there is a pervasive sense that things can only get worse, that the future is bleak.

Yearning for Balance demonstrates that, in the nation that epitomises growth fetishism, the growth project has for the most part failed to improve people's lives. It is not simply that other trends in society, occurring in parallel with rising incomes, have offset the benefits of wealth: the process of economic growth itself has produced a seriously sick society. The richest people in the world are saying they are miserable, that it's not worth it and, most disturbingly of all, that the process of getting rich *causes* the problems. Continued pursuit of material acquisition gives rise to inner conflicts that become manifest in society in various ways. At the level of the individual, some religious groups and popular gurus attempt to reconcile acquisitiveness and religious belief: 'God wants you to be rich'. For Christians, this takes some work, given the Bible's unambiguous statements about the effects of wealth: 'The love of money is the root of all evil'; 'It is easier for a camel to go through the eye of a needle, than for a rich man to enter into the kingdom of God'; 'For what shall it profit a man, if he shall gain the whole world, and lose his own soul?'. Because they look so uncomfortable doing so, devotees of this peculiar late 20th century theology of acquisitiveness display its implausibility whenever they talk about it. Other people pretend that their real interest is in something for the benefit of humankind, such as advancing information technology, and that wealth is an accidental by-product they can take or leave.

Others do not attempt to reconcile wealth with purity but investigate ways of cultivating the deeper aspects of themselves. This explains the proliferation of self-help books, a publishing phenomenon in itself. It is easy to be dismissive of this trend because the books, often written by unctuous self-styled gurus, are full of pop psychology, false promises and superficiality. But the *Yearning for Balance* report suggests that the self-help movement represents something important—the search for meaning beyond the world of consumption; the recognition, if only subliminally, that the socially sanctioned recipe for contentment is a sham. Although one might ask what such people are searching for, a more interesting question to ask is why a larger number of people appear not to be making any attempt to resolve the contradiction. Like Jack Nicholson's rebellious character 'Mack' in *One Flew over the Cuckoo's Nest*, at least those in the self-help movement are *trying;* at least they are looking for another way, rather than succumbing to the deadening security of the consumer asylum. But of course self-help can go only so far. The growth fetish is the product of a social structure that skews the priorities of individuals. Just as we will not solve our environmental problems by appealing to voluntary action by enlightened individuals, the answer to the growth fetish is political.

Political implications

One of the more subtle effects of the rise of neoliberalism is the way this school of thought has countered popular views about the distribution of power in society. For neoliberals, the enemy of freedom is collectivism and the power of the state. They argue that free markets and competition quite properly give power to individuals because only individuals can make choices about what is in their interests. The individual is not the citizen but the consumer, and for the consumer to be powerful everything must be brought into the realm of the market. Of course, 'empowering the consumer' means entrenching inequality because the power of consumers is directly proportional to their incomes. Empowering the consumer provides the rationale for the commodification of everything, including education, the natural environment and government services. But in societies restructured on neoliberal principles, it is not really the consumers who are served by the shift in power. The shift in power serves those who acquire more power as the influence of government is pared back—the corporations and the financial markets. In fact, neoliberalism takes power from individuals because, whereas previously individuals had power in the market as well as power as citizens acting in the political process, now they have power only in the market. But the power of choice in the marketplace is no power at all. Indeed, as is shown in subsequent chapters, the individual becomes a victim of the forces of the market.

In practice, growth fetishism has been responsible for a historic transfer of political authority from the state to the private market. If growth is the path to greater national and personal wellbeing, should not those responsible for growth be encouraged at every opportunity? Growth fetishism therefore cedes enormous political power to business, and corporations are never reluctant to argue that, since they are creators of wealth, it is their interests that should be paramount for government. In any political debate, whether it be about health funding, rail privatisation, greenhouse policies or a new freeway, those who argue that a certain decision will facilitate investment immediately have the upper hand. Only when the social costs of more investment are obvious and overwhelming—for example, mining in a national park or the health damage caused by further investment in tobacco production—might governments step in to oppose 'development'.

The enormous growth in global financial markets consolidated the argument that the markets are irresistible, so it would be folly to resist. The process was largely completed by the end of the 1980s. The fall of the Berlin Wall in 1989 drove home the message that the Left had lost its raison d'être.[12] While the Left in the West was traditionally too moderate, and too committed to political and civil liberties, to support socialism as practised in Eastern Europe, the Soviet bloc had nevertheless tempered the excesses of capitalism and served as a bulwark against the final triumph of US corporate capitalism.

Governments of all persuasions are now mesmerised by economic growth and find it awkward to think about national progress more broadly. Growth, investment, development, competitiveness, free trade—these aspects of the market system are powerful political symbols, before which political parties of the Left and Right kneel. In the last 25 years, politics in the West has been marked by the ideological convergence of the main parties. The process has been one in which social democrats have abandoned their traditional commitments and converged on the free-market policies of the conservatives. It is now a commonplace to observe that the conservatives, seeing their political ground occupied by the parties of the Left, have purified their neoliberalism, discarded the old ideas of social conservatism, and moved further to the Right. But this process is now starting to turn in on itself. In one state of Australia, for instance, when the conservative party installed a moderate to replace a right-wing leader who had lost two elections, a party official observed that they had not been able to outflank the Labor government from the Right, so it was time to try to do so from the Left.[13]

The convergence of social democratic politics on Thatcherism was possible because the fundamental goal of both social democracy and Thatcherism had become the same—more growth—and once the socialist method of attaining more growth lost credibility there was nowhere else to go. In fact, these trends provided conservative thinkers such as Francis Fukuyama with the raw material for a grand theory of convergence:

> . . . while earlier forms of government were characterized by grave defects and irrationalities that led to their eventual collapse, liberal democracy [is] arguably free from such fundamental internal contradictions . . . [I]t makes sense . . . to speak of a coherent and directional History of mankind that will eventually lead the greater part of humanity to liberal democracy.[14]

The political implications of the ideological convergence that occurred during the 1980s and 1990s have been profound. While the technocratic elites were rewarded ever more generously by the markets, for many working people the benefits of growth became more elusive: incomes at the bottom stagnated, unemployment rose, and working hours became longer. But, with the exception of Japan, even in the less stable economic environment of the 1980s growth resumed and consumption preoccupied the masses as never before.

As a result of these changes, and especially the convergence of the political parties, the political culture of Western democracies has been transformed. The blame for this must be laid principally at the feet of the social democratic and labour parties. People no longer know what the parties of the Left stand for. The policies of these parties no longer resonate. Party loyalty has been eroded because the sense of class solidarity that once defined the parties of the Left has evaporated. The more the parties converge in substance, the more they must attempt to differentiate themselves through 'spin'. The politics of spin are the politics of falsity, and there is a popular belief that the democratic process has become an elaborate charade. The major parties, now dominated by careerists, become frenzied about trivial things, lashing out at their opponents with declarations of outrage while tacitly agreeing not to break the neoliberal consensus on what really matters. No wonder people feel alienated and political space is created for the emergence of parties of the far Right. The irony is that, instead of blaming the system and the operators who benefit from it, some who become alienated turn their bitterness on those least able to protect themselves—single mothers, immigrants and indigenous people, for example.

Growth fetishism and its handmaiden neoliberalism thus undermine democracy. They have eroded democratic practice and democratic awareness in ordinary people. Social democracy is being superseded by a sort of market totalitarianism. When older people bemoan the corruption of modern politics, they nevertheless feel that it is a historical aberration impinging on the constancy of democratic rights and that in the end the people can still have their say. Disturbingly, younger people hear only the accusation that the system is incurably corrupt—and they believe it.

2

Growth and wellbeing

Income

Considering modern societies' obsession with economic growth, it is surprising how little attention is paid in public debate and political discourse to the question of whether more economic growth actually increases wellbeing. Perhaps this avoidance is convenient for those who have a stake in the prevailing system: if growth does not improve wellbeing, many of the economic, social and political structures of advanced capitalism cannot be justified. Perhaps ordinary people too have a stake in ignoring the evidence on growth's effects on wellbeing. When people are persuaded that more income will make them happier, they typically react to the disappointment that follows the attainment of that income by concluding that they simply do not have enough. This is a cycle without end—hope followed by disappointment followed by hope—unless some event or sudden realisation breaks it.

In fact, there is now a large body of evidence that casts serious doubt on the dual assumptions that more economic growth improves social wellbeing and that more income improves individual wellbeing. It is a body of evidence systematically ignored by policy makers and most economists, yet it is consistent with folk knowledge, accumulated through the ages, that money cannot buy a happy life. Not only does the evidence cast doubt on the growth assumption; it also points to the factors that do contribute to individual and social wellbeing. Although many of the factors that cause people to be more or less happy are beyond the influence of governments or communities, some of them are not. From a policy point of view, if we know what improves wellbeing we can know better what to emphasise. We know that there is a general assumption that increasing people's incomes will make them happier and that as a result increasing the rate of economic growth is vitally important. But the question, even in economic terms, is much more complex. If rising incomes result in increasing happiness then we would expect three relationships to hold:

- People in richer countries will be happier than people in poorer countries.
- Within each country, rich people will be happier than poor people.
- As people become richer they will also become happier.

What is the evidence for each of these? While acknowledging that part of the problem is the way in which consumer society has redefined our understanding of happiness, for the time being we assume that the meanings of 'happiness' and 'life satisfaction' are understood.

To start to answer these questions, a number of studies have compared average levels of reported life satisfaction across countries with varying levels of national income per person. At the national level, there is a weak positive correlation between a country's income and self-reported life satisfaction. This relationship may, however, be due to factors other than national income but that are themselves correlated with national income—such as the presence of political freedom and democracy, and tolerance of difference. Some evidence also suggests a negative relationship between income and happiness. For example, within Asia, residents of wealthy countries such as Japan and Taiwan regularly report the highest proportion of unhappy people, while the countries with the lowest incomes, such as the Philippines, report the highest number of happy people.[1]

Table 1 shows reported levels of 'average appreciation of life', on a scale of 0 to 1, for a selection from 48 nations for which data are available. Measures of life satisfaction are based on self-reported perceptions of happiness. The first column shows the 'happiness' ranking of each country. The figures on average appreciation of life apply to the early 1990s. The other columns show real GDP per capita in 1994 and the Human Development Index, an index constructed by the United Nations Development Program that includes measures of life expectancy and education levels as well as per capita incomes.

**Table 1   Appreciation of life, GDP and Human Development Index:
selected countries, early 1990s**

Appreciation of life Ranking	Country	Average appreciation of life, early 1990s	GDP per capita (US$PPP)[a] 1994	HDI 1994
1	Netherlands	0.797	19 238	0.940
2	Iceland	0.793	20 556	0.942
3	Denmark	0.787	21 341	0.927
7	Australia	0.767	19 285	0.931
10	United Kingdom	0.760	18 260	0.931
11	United States	0.760	26 397	0.942
12	Norway	0.743	21 346	0.943
16	France	0.720	20 510	0.946
18	Philippines	0.693	2681	0.672
20	Argentina	0.690	8937	0.884
21	Canada	0.683	21 459	0.960
22	Germany	0.680	19 675	0.924
25	Japan	0.666	21 581	0.940
26	Italy	0.660	19 363	0.921
30	Nigeria	0.643	1351	0.393
31	China	0.640	2604	0.626
33	South Korea	0.620	10 656	0.890
36	India	0.603	1348	0.446
43	Russia	0.510	4828	0.792
46	Belarus	0.487	4713	0.806
47	Bulgaria	0.433	4533	0.780

a. Exchange rates converted to US$ at purchasing power parity.

Sources: Appreciation of life—A. Wearing & B. Headey, 'Who Enjoys Life and Why? Measuring Subjective Well-being', in Richard Eckersley (ed.), *Measuring Progress. Is Life Getting Better?* (CSIRO Publishing, Collingwood), Table 1; GDP and HDI–UNDP, Human Development Index (<www.undp.org/hdro/98hdi.htm>)

The figures suggest that Dutch people are the happiest in the world and Bulgarians the most miserable. Perhaps the Bulgarians are naturally lugubrious, or perhaps the survey was done during a dark chapter in their history. It is apparent that, while there is a tendency for wealthier nations to be higher on the scale of appreciation of life, there are many cases where a country with a much lower per capita GDP ranks higher than countries with much higher per capita GDP. The correlation between the two is not strong.[2] If we take the top 17 ranked countries, with per capita incomes ranging from $16 000 to $34 000 (not all shown in Table 1), there is no relationship at all between higher incomes and higher reported appreciation of life.[3] Another study indicates that there is a threshold level of around US$10 000 above which a higher average income makes no difference to a population's reported life satisfaction.[4] As noted, Table 1 also lists the 1994 Human Development Index for a selection from the 48 countries (for the early 1990s). Perhaps surprisingly, this index—one that includes measures of education and life expectancy as well as income—does not do any better than GDP as a proxy for appreciation of life.[5]

Overall, the figures suggest that it is unlikely that in itself additional income makes much difference to wellbeing in developed countries. Other social researchers have tried to relate levels of subjective wellbeing to various characteristics of a nation. Among the factors associated with higher levels of happiness are knowledge, industrialisation, civil rights and tolerance. Among the factors associated with lower levels of happiness are unsafe drinking water, the murder rate, corruption, lethal accidents and gender inequality.[6] These suggest priorities for government policies and changes to the social structure that would put increasing the growth rate of GDP well down on the list.

Obviously, income matters a great deal for people living in poverty. There are powerful arguments for more economic growth in countries where a large proportion of the populace lives in poverty. But this should not be construed as an unalloyed endorsement of growth at all costs. The nature of the growth process matters. Increases in average income often conceal widening inequality, and in countries undergoing industrialisation large numbers of people are thrown out of rural impoverishment into a worse condition in the informal economies of the cities. In addition, millions of people who have climbed their way out of poverty have been plunged back into it by economic collapse, with no safety net and in an even more parlous situation than when they had a plot of land to fall back on. When a nation is above the threshold below which increasing income does improve wellbeing, it is no longer persuasive to argue that more growth is needed to conquer residual poverty. Rich nations have been rich for a long time but the residual poverty has become intractable. Indeed, in most industrialised nations (and certainly the Anglophone ones), by some measures poverty rates have risen in the last two decades despite the fact that incomes have continued to grow.

The question of the relationship between inequality and improvements in wellbeing is less clear-cut than that of the relationship between poverty and growth. In general, more equal societies are more happy societies. In a review of the evidence, Michael Argyle notes studies that conclude that income equality is a stronger predictor of national happiness than income levels.[7] There are two sets of reasons for believing this. First, a body of evidence shows that, with respect to income, people judge their wellbeing not by the absolute amount of their income but by its relative level. Thus psychological wellbeing is shown to depend not on one's level of income but on the perceived gap between one's actual and desired income, one's actual and expected income, and one's actual income and the incomes of others.[8] Richard Easterlin, who did much of the early work in this field, referred to a 'hedonic treadmill', on which people have to keep running in order to keep up with the others, but they never go forward. Thus, even if rich people were significantly happier than people with moderate incomes, this does not mean that raising the incomes of the latter group would make them happier. If the rich have become richer still, no one is better off. The rich would need to become less rich. Other studies suggest that, as incomes rise, income and economic factors become less important in welfare. This has been described by the British economist Sir John Hicks as the 'law of diminishing marginal significance of economics'.[9] The second reason is that more equal societies are happier societies because even in rich countries inequality itself has been shown to be associated with increased ill-health. It seems hard to sustain the view that people in richer countries are happier than people in poorer countries.

What of our second question: Are rich people happier than poor people? There is evidence from an array of studies relating individual or household incomes to levels of happiness or wellbeing. The evidence shows that, beyond a certain point, increased income does not result in increased wellbeing.[10] In other words, the rich do not appear to be happier than those who have a moderate level of income. The direct evidence on the relationship between income levels and happiness is extensive.[11] In the

United States there is virtually no difference in reported satisfaction between people with incomes of $20 000 and $80 000. In Switzerland the highest income group reports a somewhat lower level of happiness than the income group just below it.[12] The poor, as opposed to those on moderate incomes, do have significantly lower levels of wellbeing than the rich, although the difference is not large. In poor countries such as Bangladesh, wealthier people have higher levels of wellbeing than poor people. But in rich countries, having more income makes surprisingly little difference.[13] A survey of the 100 people on the Forbes list of wealthiest Americans, each with a net worth exceeding $100 million, found only slightly higher levels of subjective wellbeing than a sample of ordinary people drawn from the telephone book. When asked about the sources of their happiness none of the wealthy group claimed that money is a major source of happiness; they more often mentioned self-esteem and self-actualisation as the sources of wellbeing.[14] According to the authors of the study, 'One fabulously wealthy man said he could never remember being happy. One woman reported that money could not undo misery caused by her children's problems. Examples of the wretched wealthy are not hard to come by—Howard Hughes, Christina Onassis, J. Paul Getty'.[15] In the United States, there are now counselling services for the rich and their children, providing advice on how to deal with the psychological damage caused by great wealth.

If more income results in more happiness we would expect a growing nation to report increasing levels of life satisfaction over time. Data for Japan show that in the period 1958 to 1991 real GDP per person increased sixfold, yet reported satisfaction with life did not change at all.[16] In the United States, where consistent surveys have been conducted since 1946, real incomes have increased by 400 per cent, yet there has been no increase in reported levels of wellbeing.[17] Indeed, the proportion of Americans reporting themselves to be 'very happy' declined from 35 per cent in 1957 to 30 per cent in 1988, while the percentage who said they agreed with the statement that they were 'pretty well satisfied with [their] financial situation' fell from 42 to 30 per cent.[18] This is astonishing: despite a trebling of real incomes during the period, fewer Americans in the 1990s are satisfied with their incomes than was the case in the 1950s. The implications of the figures cannot be brushed aside: if a sharp rise in personal incomes does not result in any increase in reported life satisfaction, why do we as societies give such enormous emphasis to economic growth?

One answer to this conundrum can be found in figures presented by Juliet Schor in her book *The Overspent American.* Schor reports that 27 per cent of households with incomes of more than $100 000 a year say they cannot afford to buy everything they really need. 'Overall, over half of the population of the richest country in the world say they cannot afford everything that they really need. And it's not just the poorer half.'[19] Moreover, more than a third of those with incomes of $50 000 to $75 000 say they spend nearly all of their income on the basic necessities of life. A similar study in Australia in 2002 found that among the richest 20 per cent of households, 46 per cent said that they could not afford everything they really need.[20] Schor also reports on a poll conducted in 1986, in which Americans were asked how much income they would need to fulfil all of their dreams.

(Notice the assumption on which the question is based.) The answer was $50 000. Eight years later the figure had risen to $102 000.

Further insight into the relationship between national income and wellbeing can be gained from a 1992 study comparing living standards in Japan and Australia.[21] Japan has a substantially higher level of per capita GNP than Australia, but does this make Japanese people better off? In the 1990s it was often pointed out that Japanese per capita income was almost the highest in the world and that for some decades other countries had been falling behind. In his analysis of Japanese and Australian living standards, Castles observed that the usual comparisons are based on estimates of real expenditure per person, so he set out to make a more comprehensive comparison of living standards in Sydney and four Japanese cities—Tokyo, Kanagawa, Kyoto and Osaka. The Japanese cities have population densities about five or six times greater than that of Sydney, and people in the Japanese cities have much less private and public space. The dwellings are less spacious than those in Sydney (75 square metres compared with 139 square metres), and they are on allotments of land only a quarter the size. The provision of public amenities—in the form of parks, roads, school grounds, hospital grounds, and sporting facilities—is much higher in Sydney than in the Japanese cities. While Japanese city dwellers enjoy around 250 hectares of public open space per million of population, Sydneysiders have over 4000 hectares, and while Japanese have 32 playing fields per million of population, Sydney residents have more than 500.

These facts have a major bearing on living standards. Another vital question concerns how much time Australians and Japanese must sacrifice in order to sustain their levels of consumption. Whereas Sydneysiders worked around 35 hours a week (males, 38.5; females, 30), Japanese city dwellers worked around 47 hours each week (males, 50.5; females, 41), suggesting that higher incomes in Japan are acquired at a high cost in terms of over-work. [22] One way to look at this is to calculate the cost of a basket of foodstuffs measured in hours of work. Whether measured in terms of either a Japanese or a Sydney basket, Japanese city dwellers must work more than twice as long as Sydneysiders. The results represent a biased picture of living standards to the extent that foodstuffs are relatively more expensive in Japan, but the cost in hours worked of most other goods and services is also higher in Japan than in Australia, although by a much narrower margin.

Castles concludes that, while the growth rate of per capita income has been much faster in Japan than in Australia for some decades, Australians 'continue to enjoy higher real consumption levels per capita, in respect of virtually every significant category of expenditure. This was true notwithstanding the facts that they worked fewer hours each week, took longer holidays and had shorter working lives'. The comparison of Japan and Australia tells us that income per person can be a very misleading indi-cator of wellbeing, even when considered only in material terms. At a minimum, we need to know the conditions under which that income was generated and the circumstances in which it is consumed. The discussion of 'the emptiness of Japanese affluence' is taken up again in Chapter 3, but the study just summarised poses the question of whether people in Japan would have been happier if they had exchanged some economic growth for more time.

On the basis of the evidence reviewed here, it is reasonable to draw the following broad conclusions: above a certain level of national income people in richer countries are no happier than people in poorer countries; in any given country rich people are no happier than those with moderate incomes; and as people become richer they do not become happier. These conclusions need to be tempered by the observation that more income does make a difference to people who are very poor and lack the basics of food, shelter and health care. But this does not change the fundamental observation that in rich countries increasing incomes through more economic growth does not improve levels of national wellbeing. Moreover, the economic structure and policies that maximise growth come at the expense of measures to improve the lot of the residual poor.

Personal happiness

A deeper understanding of the aetiology of happiness can be gained by considering the relationship between levels of happiness and the personal characteristics of people. There is an extensive psychological literature on this question. Myers and Diener summarise the results from a large number of studies and conclude that there are four traits characteristic of happy people.[23] First, they have high levels of self-esteem and usually 'believe themselves to be more ethical, more intelligent, less prejudiced, better able to get along with others, and healthier than the average person'. Second, they tend to feel more in control of their lives. Those with little control—those trapped in poverty and citizens living under authoritarian regimes—tend to be more despondent and less healthy. Third, happy people tend to be more optimistic. Fourth, they are more extroverted.

More detailed research has broken down the variation in happiness levels between individuals into several components. Personal psychological factors (such as those just mentioned) explain 30 per cent of the variation in levels of happiness. Life events such as divorce, the birth or death of a child, and illness account for a further 25 per cent. Social participation, including voluntary activities, paid work and marriage, account for another 10 per cent. It is surprising to discover that income and material wealth account for only about 10 per cent of the variation in personal levels of happiness.[24]

Further evidence on the chimerical effect of wealth is provided by studies of lottery winners. A study of winners of major lotteries found that they were no happier than a control sample but that they took significantly less pleasure in mundane events.[25] Although there is an immediate lift in mood, the euphoria is temporary and activities that previously gave pleasure, such as reading, may become less pleasurable. Summarising this research, Myers quotes the author of these studies—'Happiness is not the result of being rich, but a temporary consequence of having recently become rich'—and notes other work that confirms that 'those whose incomes have increased over a 10-year period are not happier than those whose income has not increased . . . Happiness is less a matter of getting what we want than of wanting what we have'.[26] On the other hand, gambling plays a powerful part in social control by promising a way of breaking out of the constraints of everyday life. For many people, living in the hope of a chance external intervention deprives them of the motivation to change their personal or community circumstances.

These studies show that, in general, social relationships, including relationships with family and friends, are the most important determinant of happiness. They also show that married people tend to be more happy than divorced (or separated) people. While unemployment is a source of great unhappiness, job satisfaction is very significant as a source of happiness, as is 'serious or committed leisure' (as opposed to passive television viewing). Religious belief is also a very important source of happiness for some. In one of the most thorough investigations of the determinants of happiness, the researchers came to a startling conclusion: 'A sense of meaning and purpose is the single attitude most strongly associated with life satisfaction'.[27] I return to this later because it demands a deeper consideration of the notions of happiness and wellbeing than has underpinned the discussion so far.

The studies described generally find that personal happiness is heavily influenced by relative factors. Personal happiness depends on what people have compared with what they want, what they expect, and what other people have. This leads naturally to an exploration of the goals people set for themselves. In other words, the determinants of happiness are not simply given and immutable—part of the human condition and therefore beyond influence by social organisation and public policies. The goals people set are strongly influenced by social expectations, which can change rapidly. A large body of psychological research shows that these goals have a major bearing on people's subjective well-being. In 1998 three psychologists reviewed the evidence:

> There is a substantial research base that demonstrates that people's priorities are prime determinants of their well-being, and that these priorities are based on their current and long-term goals, projects and concerns . . . The goals people strive for, the manner in which they strive for them, and their ability to integrate the goals into a reasonably coherent framework influence their subjective well-being.[28]

The psychologists reported that people whose goals emphasise intimacy and affiliation with others (reflecting 'a concern for establishing deep and mutually gratifying relationships') have higher levels of wellbeing than those whose goals emphasise power (reflecting a desire to have an impact and influence on others). Statistically, the associations between types of strivings and wellbeing are only modest. However, conflict between personal goals—a situation in which attainment of a primary goal interferes with the ability to attain another goal—is strongly related to diminished wellbeing. Trying to spend more time with one's family while doing well in one's career is a good example of a goal conflict that will cause distress, especially if the conflict becomes chronic and is associated with poorer psychological health and physical ill-health.

In a series of studies, some published in leading journals, Kasser and Ryan distinguish between two sets of beliefs about the sources of happiness.[29] The first is the belief that the path to happiness lies in the pursuit of the external goals of wealth, fame and physical attractiveness. The second is that happiness grows from striving for deeper relationships and personal growth and from contributing to the community. The first set of beliefs is a self-focused system, one in which happiness is derived from extrinsic material rewards. Clearly, this is the modern myth of the consumer society: we are bombarded daily with images and messages that try to persuade us that we can find contentment and fulfilment by acquiring this product or that one or by pursuing a perfect body image or clawing our way up the corporate ladder. Thus we celebrate the wealthy, the powerful, the famous and the beautiful.

After classifying individuals according to whether they operate on the basis of a belief in extrinsic goals (money, fame and beauty) or intrinsic goals (relationships and personal growth), the researchers then ask which group is happier. The conclusions, summarised by Tim Kasser, are unambiguous: 'Individuals oriented towards materialistic, extrinsic goals are more likely to experience lower quality of life than individuals oriented toward intrinsic goals'. But the news gets worse. Not only are those with extrinsic orientation in life less happy than those with intrinsic goals; they make others less happy too:

> Further, extrinsically oriented individuals are shown to have shorter, more conflictual, and more competitive relationships with others, thus impacting the quality of life of those around them. In sum, the pursuit of personal goals for money, fame and attractiveness is shown to lead to a lower quality of life than the goals of relatedness, self-acceptance and community feeling.

The four traits of happy people that Myers and Diener identified—self-esteem, control over one's life, optimism and extroversion—are also associated with close personal relationships. People who can name several intimate friends are healthier and happier than those who have few or no close friends. As noted, married people tend to be happier than unmarried people, although there is a risk of a period of great unhappiness if the marriage founders. In the United States around 40 per cent of married people say they are 'very happy', while only around 25 per cent of those who have never married report being very happy.

These studies confirm what many people know intuitively— that the goals of wealth, fame and attractiveness are hollow. They show that when people pursuing these goals achieve them they do not feel any better as a result. Indeed, the research shows that people who have extrinsic goals tend to be more depressed than others, and they suffer from higher levels of psychological disturbance as well as scoring lower on measures of vitality and self-awareness. One study found that teenagers in a high-risk group who put great stress on financial success were less likely to contribute to their communities and more likely to engage in antisocial behaviour such as muggings and vandalism. Another study found that extrinsically oriented individuals had briefer, more narcissistic relationships and their romantic attachments were marked by more jealousy and less trust: 'This is a particularly poignant finding, especially when one considers that behind an extrinsically oriented individual's behavior may lie a desire to be loved and admired'.[30] On the other hand, those who have intrinsic goals concentrated on closer relationships, self-development and helping others improve their levels of wellbeing as they attain their goals. Although this research program focused on the United

States, the results are beginning to be replicated in other cultures, notably Germany, Russia and India.

The researchers provide further insight into the relationship between goals and wellbeing. Longitudinal studies show that people who make progress towards reaching intrinsic goals experience improved wellbeing, while those who attain their extrinsic goals are no happier.[31] In other words, if our relationships improve we become happier, but if our bank balance grows we do not. Moreover, people who invest themselves in the external goals of wealth and fame are distracted from attending to their intrinsic needs and find themselves in situations characterised by 'more ego-involved, controlling and competitive settings that themselves can 'undermine' intrinsic satisfactions'. In an observation with profound implications for consumer societies, Kasser and Ryan write:

> Procuring externally visible outcomes that convey 'outer' worth thus may reflect a compensatory attempt to obtain a sense of 'inner' worth . . . [One study showed] that adolescents who were more materialistic came from maternal-care environments that were less nurturant . . . environments characterized by cold, controlling maternal care.

I explore the relationship between family structure and consumption habits later. Kasser and Ryan also show that individuals with extrinsic orientation use drugs, cigarettes and alcohol more frequently and that these may be a form of self-medication to cope with their less satisfying lives or lower self-esteem.[32] It is also apparent that levels of television watching are especially related to extrinsic goals, a relationship that may be explained by television's role as a stress reliever or its power to induce a greater orientation to goals of wealth and fame. There is experimental evidence to support the latter interpretation.

The authors of these studies—staid, careful psychologists—draw a radical conclusion, one that presents no threat as long as it remains safely confined to the academic literature: 'Thus it appears that the suggestion within American culture that well-being and happiness can be found through striving to become rich, famous, and attractive may themselves be chimerical'.[33]

The implications of this research for public policy and social development could not be more far-reaching. The results strongly suggest that the more our media, advertisers and opinion makers emphasise financial success as the chief means to happiness the more they promote social pathologies. This is why the researchers gave their papers such titles as 'Be Careful What You Wish For' and 'A Dark Side of the American Dream'.

Although the citizens of rich countries have attained unprecedented levels of personal wealth, they are also afflicted by an epidemic of psychological disorders. According to one study, depression has increased tenfold among Americans born since the Second World War.[34] Young people, the principal beneficiaries of super-affluence, are most prone to clinical depression, evidenced in record rates of teenage suicide and other social pathologies such as self-destructive drug taking. The risk of major depression is two or three times higher among women than among men, but the gap is closing because of the faster increase in the incidence of depression among young males. These trends are evident across rich Western countries—including the United

States, Canada, Sweden, Germany and New Zealand—but not in Korea or Puerto Rico.[35]

According to the World Health Organization and the World Bank, the burden of psychiatric conditions has been greatly underestimated. Of the ten leading causes of disability worldwide in 1990 (measured in years lived with a disability), five were psychiatric disorders—major depression (the number one cause), alcohol use (fourth), bipolar disorder (sixth), schizophrenia (ninth) and obsessive-compulsive disorders (tenth).[36] Major depression is responsible for more than one in ten of all years lived with a disability. The burden is greater in, but by no means restricted to, the rich countries. While major depression is already the leading cause of disability worldwide, when measured in terms of disability-adjusted life-years it is expected to leap from being the fourth most burdensome disease in the world in 1990 to second place in 2020. In rich countries, one out of every four disability-adjusted life-years is lost due to psychiatric disorders, which is an astounding burden of mental ill-health. In developing countries, psychiatric disorders are fast replacing traditional infectious diseases as the leading causes of ill-health.

Reflecting a 19th century preoccupation with mortality rates, the critical role of neuropsychiatric disorders in community well-being has been ignored because they are absent from the list of causes of death. Moreover, psychiatric disorders are frequently misdiagnosed and improperly treated as physical disorders because of the general social fixation on correcting deviations from a happy ideal rather than acknowledging widespread social distress. Mental health care does not generally require sophisticated equipment and invasive medicine; it requires properly trained, suitable professionals with plenty of time to deal with each patient.

Although researchers have been effective at mapping the increasing incidence of major depression, they have been unable to explain it. They identify vague risk factors (including in one case 'being a female adolescent') but are yet to explore them. It is known that a person's chances of suffering from depression are greater if they are impoverished, unemployed or living in a dysfunctional family, if they have been abused as a child, or if they have a family history of mental illness. Other studies suggest broader social changes that probably get closer to a social explanation and avoid focusing on problems with individuals. They mention urbanisation, geographic mobility, changes in family structure, and the changing roles of women. But one factor stands out in the discussion of the aetiology of depression and solutions to it: social isolation. The erosion of social connectedness—manifested in loss of face-to-face contact, the change in family structures, the transformation of workplaces, and the commercialisation of community activities such as sport—and the consequent deterioration of relationship skills lie at the heart of the epidemic of mental illness. The problem then becomes how to explain it. What *is* the explanation for the erosion of social connectedness and the pervasive loneliness of modern societies?

People who are obsessed by the accumulation of wealth necessarily focus on their own circumstances and those of their immediate family. Focusing on one's own perceived needs means an inward psychological orientation, so that the needs of others fade into the background. Moreover, the pursuit of wealth is inherently competitive: success demands that one elbow out rivals; one's own superiority depends on the inferiority of others. People who pursue wealth put themselves under time pressure, so that they lack time to devote to activities that build communities, including simple activities such as talking to neighbours and taking an interest in the rest of the world and its travails. Finally, people who are preoccupied with money and material acquisition have a psychological affinity with things rather than with relationships, and their relationships are more likely to be structured so as to assist the quest for accumulation. Relationships with family, friends and the wider community are mediated through materialist objectives. This is the story of postwar consumer capitalism.

Depression is not the only unexplained psychological disorder in wealthy societies. Increasing numbers of people are easily distracted, find it difficult to concentrate on the task before them, have difficulty listening to what is being said, talk too much, cannot sit still for more than a few minutes, and are drawn to physically dangerous activities without considering the possible consequences. In fact, these are the signs listed by the American Psychiatric Association as characterising attention deficit disorder (also known as attention deficit/hyperactivity disorder). Rates of diagnosis of ADD in the United States grew extraordinarily in the 1990s. No one knows what 'causes' this disease, which predominantly affects white middle-class boys, but there is a suspicion that 'toxins, environmental problems, or neurological immaturity' could be responsible.

The response to ADD says as much about the modern world as the rise of the disorder itself. The answer has been drug therapy. Prescription of Ritalin, a powerful stimulant derived from the cocaine family, increased by 700 per cent in the United States between 1990 and 1999, with between 4 and 5 million children taking the drug regularly. In some schools, 20 per cent of fifth-grade boys take daily doses of Ritalin and—in an eerie reminder of mental hospital routine—teachers line up bottles of medication, clearly marked by name, so that children can be doped to get through the day. Ritalin masks some of the symptoms of ADD and has given rise to side effects known as 'Ritalin rebound', including weight loss, insomnia, facial tics and a 'sense of sadness'. It is increasingly used as a recreational drug by teenagers and college students, who refer to it as 'vitamin R'. Crushed and snorted like cocaine, it gives a rush and helps when cramming for exams.

Although a small number of children do require drug therapy, the boom in prescription of Ritalin reflects expectations of children in a society in the grip of the growth fetish. Lawrence Diller, a physician whose book *Running on Ritalin* exposes the misuse of the drug, links the frequency of diagnosis of ADD and the explosion in prescription of Ritalin to social changes in the community. Classrooms and child-care centres are now pressure environments. In the 1970s only 30 per cent of mothers of young children worked outside the home; now over 70 per cent do, and both parents work harder at jobs that are often less secure. Diller suggests that normal children who are simply inattentive or bored with school or who are prone to daydreaming or slow at finishing their chores at home are brought into doctors' surgeries by hyped-up parents, willingly diagnosed as having a chemical disorder of the brain, and prescribed a powerful drug. The rates of Ritalin prescription vary enormously from one community to the next but are much higher in white middle-class communities, where Ritalin has become a sort of performance-enhancing drug that would be illegal in sport. 'American psychiatry which used to blame Johnny's mother for his behavior problems now blames Johnny's brain.'[37] Diller offers a Swiftian 'modest proposal': 'With classroom sizes now averaging about 30 kids per class and about four million children taking Ritalin, I propose we increase the number of children taking Ritalin to seven million and we could probably increase class sizes to 45 children and save a lot of money'.

When doctors reach for their prescription pads they send a series of powerful messages, especially to children. Deviations from the norm, defined increasingly by the imperatives of commerce and the need to secure employment, are medical conditions and the answer is to take drugs to fix them. Trying to understand who you are and how you fit into social structures is a waste of time because the problem is neurological. Reconciling your emotional responses is not something you do through relationships with other human beings and self-understanding; you do it by correcting your faults through outside intervention. As Diller puts it, a 'living imbalance' has become a 'neurochemical imbalance', and at a time when we are no longer willing to intimidate children into compliance we are willing to drug them into it. It is difficult to avoid the parallel with the Soviet Union's use of psychiatry as a device for controlling political dissidents.

A society obsessed with 'making it'—in which the markers of success demand extraordinary commitment to paid employment—has little time to nurture its children with the care they require and deserve. Once a part of the age-old process of reproducing and attaining emotional fulfilment as an adult, children are increasingly expressions of their parents' preoccupations and abstract desires. Thus they become an encumbrance. The 'epidemic' of ADD says more about the changing structure of families, absentee parents, crippling pressure to succeed, a culture of winners and losers, and economies that are ever richer but can devote no more resources to education than it does about brain chemistry. It says more about drug companies' manipulation of the medical profession and parental demands for instant fixes for children deemed deviant. The ADD craze and Ritalin are making children sick, but society would sooner believe that behavioural problems are caused by neurological disease than confront its own sickness. In this way no one is to blame—not the parents, not the education system, not family structures, not social expectations, not changes in work patterns, and not the pursuit of wealth.

Values and meaning

As already discussed, in one of the most systematic statistical analyses of the relationship between self-reported happiness and personal characteristics, the researchers came to a disquieting conclusion: 'A sense of meaning and purpose is the single attitude most strongly associated with life satisfaction'.[38] In contrast with the other factors that have been related to variations in perceived wellbeing—extroversion, goal orientation, personal circumstances such as marriage, and especially income—a focus on a sense of meaning and purpose in life demands a more careful examination of the notion of wellbeing.

The evidence reviewed so far could be criticised for undue empiricism—that is, for being too occupied with measuring happiness and its influences, to the exclusion of a deeper consideration of the nature of wellbeing and the human condition. Philosophers, playwrights and sages have been investigating the fundamental question of human happiness and its determinants for millennia, and they have done so without any recourse to empirical studies other than day-to-day observation of their social milieus. Yet these thinkers have enriched our understanding enormously. The proof of their ideas lies in the ideas' intuitive plausibility, rather than any validation against the data. In the end, most people will be motivated to accept a new way of thinking about life and social change (such as that advocated in this book) not by the accretion of scientific evidence that contradicts their beliefs but because those beliefs become untenable when confronted by the evidence of their own senses and their understanding of society around them. Despite this recognition of the unimportance of formal empirical evidence, it does remain true in our society that even the most obvious must be backed by dispassionate evidence—if only because those who benefit from denying the obvious will challenge the critic.

Most studies of happiness and its determinants have focused on positive and negative affect (emotions or feelings) and the longer term idea of life satisfaction. In other words, happiness or wellbeing is conceived of as the outcome of events that influence the senses or the self-perceived state. This notion of happiness is generally measured by 'subjective wellbeing', based on individuals' responses to questioning. One implication of thinking of happiness in this way is that it can be consistent with a hedonistic, shallow approach to life, in which questions of values and meaning are reduced to short-term emotional highs and lows. So far, the discussion has been based on the assumption that the objective of humans is to increase their level of happiness and that social organisation and practical politics should be directed towards this aim, or at least to providing the environment in which people can pursue happiness. This premise in itself concedes a great deal to the economic way of thinking and, more broadly, to the thrust of liberal political thought. But this is a modern and rather superficial conception of what it is to be human. Freud used to complain that his American acolytes had interpreted his psychotherapeutic ideas as a technique for making people happy. Steeped in European philosophical tradition, Freud believed this to be a trivialisation of a movement whose purpose was to understand the *meaning* of what people do and what their behaviour tells us about the human condition. The purpose of life is not to be happy; it is to understand ourselves so that we can achieve personal integration or reconciliation with our selves. It is a process rather than a final state.

Despite his split with Freud, Carl Jung was in accord. For him the purpose of life, and the role of psychotherapy, was to bring the conscious and unconscious minds into harmony and so find wholeness, a process he called 'individuation'. The approach of Freud and Jung grew out of a much longer tradition, one stretching back to the Greeks. Aristotle discussed happiness using the term *eudaimonia*. As Carol Ryff observes, the Greeks used *daimon* to mean genius, and in its original use the word 'genius' referred to the spirit assigned to each person at birth to preside over their destiny. *Eudaimonia* thus means good fortune in life, but Ryff prefers to describe *daimon* as 'an ideal in the sense of an excellence, a perfection towards which one strives, and which gives meaning and direction to one's life'.[39] Cast in this light, the pursuit of wellbeing becomes something associated less with day-to-day gratification and more with the evolution of a life, of the potential within each person, and of the ethical principles that underpin right behaviour, an idea that has as much resonance in Buddhist as in Christian thought.

This deeper notion of wellbeing is consistent with psychological theories that identify human lives as the unfolding of potential, notably Maslow's idea of self-actualisation as well as Jung's central concept of individuation. From this perspective, stages of life and of maturity become important for self-understanding, and wellbeing becomes identified with positive psychological functioning rather than a snapshot of a person's emotional state. The question of happiness must be understood in terms of a person's progress towards self-actualisation, or individuation; that is, approaching a state of psychological maturity in which, among other things, unconscious drives and motivations are being brought to light and made consistent with conscious life goals and principles. From this perspective, happiness is recast as inner contentment—sitting easily with whom one is—rather than a state of more or less positive emotion. The dimensions of psychological wellbeing may be described as 'self-actualisers'. They include self-acceptance; the ability to maintain warm, trusting and loving relationships; being free of social and cultural pressures to conform in ways that are inconsistent with inner standards; having a clear sense of personal direction and purpose in life; and being in a state of growth and realisation of potential.[40]

The question arises as to whether this is just a complex way of getting at whatever it is that the simple indicators of life satisfaction measure. This question lends itself to empirical investigation. Ryff's study of the meaning of wellbeing indicates that there is a high correlation between measures of generalised self-reported life satisfaction and some dimensions of self-actualisation (notably self-acceptance, environmental mastery and purpose in life) but only a weak association with others (positive relations with other people, autonomy and personal growth). Using the standard measures of wellbeing, women show up as being less happy than men, but using the broader conception of wellbeing provides a more balanced view because women score relatively well on factors such as interpersonal relationships. The research suggests that measures of short-term affective wellbeing may disguise changes in the longer term and a deeper need to realise one's potential and one's life purpose. Indeed, as is argued in the next chapter, 20th century consumer capitalism has seen a progressive substitution of activities and desires that result in immediate stimulation for the more challenging and potentially more fulfilling demands of realising one's potential. There are, then, trade-offs that must be made between short-term gratification and attaining deeper goals of self-realisation, so that it may indeed be necessary to make oneself miserable in order to acquire the understanding needed to become 'happy'.

This more subtle understanding of wellbeing provides a way into another important but neglected body of research, one that investigates the relationship between happiness and religion. In their overview of this research, Emmons and colleagues observe that religious commitment and participation consistently appear as significant contributors to life satisfaction. However, not all religious commitment is equally valuable, and some forms can be harmful to wellbeing:

> At a minimum, critical distinctions need to be made between extrinsic (religion as a means to an end) and intrinsic (religion as a way of life) religiousness, with measures of the former generally showing negative correlations with well-being and measures of the latter showing positive correlations with well-being.[41]

Even this distinction—remarkably similar to the secular one made by Kasser and Ryan—fails to reflect the complexity and depth of spirituality since 'spirituality, as typically defined, encompasses a search for meaning, for unity, for connectedness, for transcendence, for the highest of human potential'.[42] This broad conceptualisation of spirituality, which Paul Tillich refers to as an 'ultimate concern', has close secular parallels in Jung's concept of individuation and Maslow's notion of self-actualisation.

The research affirms that higher forms of spirituality contribute more to contentment than the rituals of church attendance and daily prayer—extrinsic manifestations of religion that may reflect nothing more than a desire for social acceptance, the internalisation of parental expectations, or an insurance policy against the possibility of an afterlife. In a conclusion that suggests that women take their religious beliefs more seriously than men do, the evidence shows that spiritual commitment in women is more likely to be associated with improved wellbeing than it is for men. One of the benefits of spirituality is that it provides an inner landscape within which other, more mundane life goals are embedded. As a consequence, spiritual striving resolves conflicts between other life goals and this conflict resolution makes for more contented souls. In sum, the studies show that spiritual striving contributes more to wellbeing than any other type of goal, including the goals of intimacy, power and symbolic immortality.

Although many people feel uncomfortable discussing spirituality in the context of political and social change—believing that questions of meaning and religion belong in another, more private realm—this compartmentalisation itself is a manifestation of the political and social structure. Consumption and materialism tend to drive out religion, and the more a society emphasises material pursuits and extrinsic motivations as the path to a happy life, the less validity it attaches to the pursuit of meaning or to life's inner evolution. This is not to suggest that we need government policies designed to increase church attendance. It is to say that modern consumer capitalism's preoccupation with calculation and a narrow form of rationality is hostile to the acknowledgment and expression of humans' deeper need for some connection with the mysterious, whether through organised religion or through more personal forms of spirituality. Karl Marx was one of the first to recognise the power of capitalism to change consciousness:

> The bourgeoisie, wherever it has got the upper hand, has
> put an end to all feudal, patriarchal, idyllic relations. It has

pitilessly torn asunder the motley feudal ties that bound man to his 'natural superiors', and has left remaining no other nexus between man and man than naked self-interest, than callous 'cash payment'. It has drowned the most heavenly ecstasies of religious fervour, of chivalrous enthusiasm, of philistine sentimentalism, in the icy waters of egotistical calculation.[43]

Modern capitalism elevates a certain form of rationality to a higher plane. Consumerism and the logic of capitalism are intensely bound up with the rationality of money. As Norman Brown observed, 'Money reflects and promotes a style of thinking which is abstract, impersonal, objective, and quantitative, that is to say, the style of thinking of modern science—and what could be more rational than that?'.[44] The early sociologists and historians of capitalism were struck by the dominance of this new and peculiar form of rationality whose influence spread from market exchange to all forms of social interaction. Like Marx, Max Weber pointed to the irrelevance of all commitments other than self-interest and the depersonalisation of social life. In the world of market relationships the inner worlds of feelings and spirituality were banished from the conscious mind and trivialised to the point where religious affiliation or expression of religious sense attracted derision. In popular culture, spiritual urges and religious convictions are disparaged, and a series of superficial arguments is advanced to prove the irrelevance and futility of religion—it causes more wars than it solves, it's a crutch for weak people, and so on. All this reflects a deeper transformation, the alienation of self from the seminal urge for meaning and the flight to the triviality of material consumption and frivolous gratification. In the end, religion is seen as 'uncool', something that says much more about modern marketing culture than about the relevance of religious striving to the human condition.

The argument here is not that wellbeing should or can be advanced through promotion of religious belief or spiritual endeavour; it is that a society that scorns intrinsic religiousness and trivialises the pursuit of meaning discards thousands of years of insight and can only suffer for it.

Alternative measures

Returning to the realm of everyday economics, it is not difficult to show that, even within the framework of market values and humans as consumption machines, the preoccupation with growth can be immiserising. On one hand, our measures of progress show that for decades things have been getting better; on the other, most people complain that society is going to the dogs. Perhaps the problem is that our measures of progress are getting it wrong. Our measure of national progress—growth in GDP or GNP—is bound inseparably to the price system. An activity is taken to contribute to our national wellbeing by virtue of the fact that, and solely to the extent that, it is produced for sale. The defining feature of prosperity has become monetary transaction. This way of measuring national wellbeing omits two large realms: the contributions to wellbeing of family and community and the contribution of the natural environment.

Both of these are vital to our wellbeing but, because their contributions lie outside the marketplace, they simply do not count.

We cannot separate the social afflictions of crime, drug abuse and youth suicide from the societal changes wrought by the market economy. Unemployment, overwork and the pervasive expectation that contentment derives from material acquisition are products of the market system and have profound effects on our welfare. The failure to establish a close relationship between economic growth and improvements in wellbeing, at least above a certain threshold, suggests that the pursuit of growth is occurring at the expense of things that really do increase people's wellbeing. This has led some to broaden the discussion of the determinants of wellbeing and attempt to build numerical alternatives to GDP as the measure of national progress. One such alternative is the Genuine Progress Indicator, also known as the Index of Sustainable Economic Welfare. Using established economic methods, the GPI incorporates a range of factors that influence wellbeing and aggregates them into a single index that can be compared directly over time with GDP. Although there are some conceptual and measurement difficulties with the alternative indicator, its construction points graphically to the glaring inadequacies of GDP as a measure of national progress.

The essential rationale of the GPI is that a measure of national wellbeing that is confined to goods and services produced for the market makes no sense. Many things people 'consume' lie outside the market yet affect their wellbeing. As this suggests, the GPI accepts the basic starting point of GDP (and economics more generally) that wellbeing is a function of consumption. This is the GPI's greatest weakness, but it nevertheless challenges those whose thinking is confined to the consumption model. Within the confines of an economic framework, the GPI attempts to get much closer than GDP to how the growth process is actually experienced by people. It does not include everything that affects wellbeing—or even everything that affects economic wellbeing. Only some aspects that lend themselves to monetary measurement are included. But just adding in a few of the factors that affect people's daily lives generates a story that is startlingly different from the official one.

The GPI has been constructed for around a dozen OECD countries and usually covers the period from the 1950s to the 1990s.[45] It incorporates more than twenty aspects of economic wellbeing that are either ignored or treated incorrectly in the official estimates of GDP. While there are many complex conceptual and measurement questions to be dealt with in compiling the new index, most of it is based on commonsense. An economy growing at 4 per cent but shedding jobs does not leave a community as well off as a similar economy growing at 4 per cent but maintaining employment. An economy that can grow at 4 per cent while minimising pollution is better than one growing at 4 per cent but polluting the air and water. Thus the GPI provides a national balance sheet that includes both the costs and the benefits of economic growth.

What are some of the principal factors included in the GPI?[46] When used as a measure of national progress, GDP implicitly assumes that the distribution of income is perfect and that it does not matter whether the richest family or the poorest family receives the extra income economic growth generates. Yet most people would agree that a growing economy contributes more to national wellbeing if poorer households receive a larger share of the new income.[47] Although the situation has varied from country to country, one of the general features of the industrialised world in the era of globalisation since the early 1970s has been a worsening of income distribution. The GPI adjusts growth in consumption by a measure of the changing distribution of income.

Much of the work that contributes to wellbeing occurs in the home and the community; examples are caring for children and the elderly, cooking meals, cleaning the house, and coaching the children's hockey team. Most of this work has traditionally been done by women and continues to be so. Because these activities lie outside the market, their contributions do not appear in the national accounts. Only when the market captures them—as with paid child care, the purchasing of fast food, and the employment of housekeepers—do they appear to add to our wellbeing, because they now have price tags. The GPI includes an estimate of the value of household and community work that falls outside the market.

Unemployment imposes costs on communities and nations well beyond the loss in economic output implied by enforced idleness. Many studies have shown that unemployment leads to a decline in health and skill levels, increased family breakdown and rising crime rates. There are often severe psychological impacts on unemployed people and their families. The GPI includes estimates of the financial costs of unemployment beyond the lost output implicit in the national accounts.

A substantial portion of the spending captured by GDP is defensive in nature; that is, it is undertaken to protect against some decline in wellbeing. For example, if a crime wave (real or imagined) induces increased expenditure on household security and insurance premiums, this spending is recorded as a positive contribution to our wellbeing in the official national accounts. In reality, these defensive expenditures are an attempt to maintain levels of security in the face of a more threatening world. The costs of crime are enormous and include not only the costs of preventing it (through 'target hardening') but also the health and repair bills for the victims of it. The GPI deducts from consumption spending crime-related defensive expenditures. Some other types of spending on health and accident repairs are also defensive in character and are deducted to obtain the GPI.

When economic growth causes depletion of stocks of natural resources and a decline in environmental quality, the national accounts either ignore the effects or treat them as a gain. The GPI attempts to assess these costs properly. While GDP counts the value of timber from native forests as a benefit and stops there, the GPI also counts the environmental costs of logging. In the GPI the damage done by greenhouse gas emissions is not ignored (and left as a problem for future generations to deal with); it is counted as a cost of economic activity in the year the gases are released into the atmosphere. The GPI also accounts for the costs of ozone depletion, water pollution, and depletion of non-renewable resources.

Figure 1 shows the results of GPI studies for the United Kingdom, the United States and Australia. Despite the differences in national circumstances, there is a very consistent and startling pattern: while GDP per capita has risen steadily since the 1950s, the more comprehensive measure of national prosperity, GPI, has

Figure 1   GPI and GDP per person: United Kingdom, United States and Australia (1950–2000)

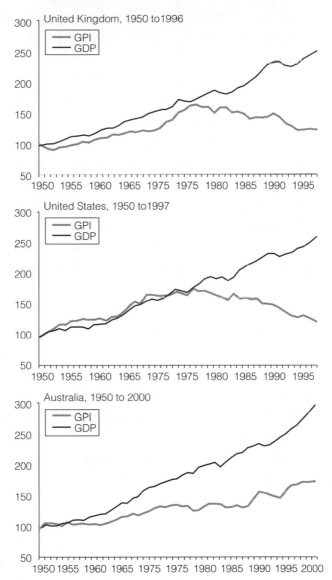

Sources: T. Jackson, N. Marks, J. Ralls and S. Stymne, *Sustainable Economic Welfare in the UK: 1950–1996*, Centre for Environmental Strategy, University of Surrey, 1997; M. Anielski and J. Rowe, *The Genuine Progress Indicator—1998 update*, Redefining Progress, San Francisco, 1999; C. Hamilton and R. Denniss, *Tracking Well-being in Australia: the Genuine Progress Indicator 2000*, Discussion Paper no. 35, The Australia Institute, Canberra, 2000.

risen much more slowly and has stagnated or declined since the 1970s. The costs of economic growth appear to have begun to outweigh the benefits. If GDP is used as a measure of national wellbeing, it must be concluded that the citizens of these countries are now much better off than they were in the 1950s and that their condition has continued to improve in each decade. If we take GDP to be a measure of national wellbeing, then young people today appear to be much better off than their parents were. But as soon as we start to add in some of the factors that are excluded from the national accounts a very different story emerges—one that helps to explain the political alienation of recent times. In each of these countries, economic growth appears to be maintained by running down the stocks of industrial capital and infrastructure as well as the stocks of social capital and natural capital, leaving gaping holes in the wealth-creation possibilities of future generations.

The new indicator is not infallible, or even an especially good measure of changes in national wellbeing, but it does challenge growth fetishism on its own terms. It uses conventional methods to demonstrate some facts that sit uneasily with the official view. The economy draws what it needs from the social realm and the natural world, and only in this way do things acquire prices so that they can be included in the national accounts. The economy spits out what it does not need—redundant workers, toxic wastes—and by this act they no longer appear in the national accounts. Contributions to our wellbeing count only if they are transferred to the market sector; the 'side effects' of the market that diminish our wellbeing are sent back to the social and environmental sectors, where they no longer count. The economy values only what it needs; what it does not need has no value.

Defenders of the growth fetish argue that aspects of life outside the economy are distinct and separate and, where they require government intervention, the policy response should not interfere with the activities of the market. But the decline of community and family life and the deterioration of the natural world are not independent of the economy: commerce, the labour market and consumerism are inseparable from their decline. Yet our measure of national wellbeing, GDP, continues to rise. If we look only at the official figures, life should be getting better. It is no longer tenable to maintain that the problems of the world beyond the market can be sliced off for separate treatment. The decline of social life and the environment must be placed at the core of the problem, growth fetishism.

3

Identity

Having and wanting

This book arose out of asking a simple but unexpectedly radical question: What makes people contented? At one level, the answer is also simple: The distance between what people have and what they want determines how contented they are. This distance—which Mishan referred to as the 'margin of discontent'—can be closed either by increasing one's possessions while keeping wants constant or by maintaining one's level of possessions and reducing one's desires. Here, the notion of 'possessions' is best thought of as the ability to have access to goods and services or, simply, income.[1]

Economic growth is usually characterised as the process whereby people satisfy their wants by increasing their possessions, thus becoming happier. But this presumption raises some awkward questions. How are people's wants determined? Is there a difference between what people say they want and what they really want? Does 'what people have' include only things that can be bought and sold? Does what people have actually satisfy them? Is what people want independent of what they have or does more 'having' drive up the level of wanting, so that the two can never meet and consumption is doomed to be a labour of Sisyphus? If so, are the sages right when they say that the only way to be happy is to give up wanting?

As is often the case, the best way to start answering these questions is to see what the economists say: deeper insight often begins from a critique of the conventional view. The neoliberal economists' view appears strange to ordinary people, but the reality is that the world is, in large measure, organised according to it. This is not so much because the economists have influenced the world (although that is certainly true); rather, it is because the economists have created a story about how the world works based on certain aspects of human behaviour—self-interested calculation, individualism and materialism. The strangeness of the economists' world arises from the fact that they recognise only this form of behaviour as valid and insist on imposing it on everything that people do.

The idea of 'consumer sovereignty' is the foundation of the economists' faith in the market and, indeed, the starting point for any challenge to economic liberalism. Neoliberal policies are based on the philosophical assumption that the right of adult individuals to make choices about how to pursue their welfare, even if they are the 'wrong' choices, is sacrosanct. This is a question of individual freedom, they argue, hence the term 'neoliberalism' (in which the ideas of classical political liberalism are extended into new realms of activity). The economists' response to the evidence presented in the last chapter would be: 'What you say may be all very well. It may be true that more money does not make people any happier. But if that is what people want, right or wrong, who are we to deny them that choice? If people cannot choose properly for themselves, no one else can do a better job'. This idea is the basis of neoliberal political philosophy, as articulated by writers such as Ayn Rand, Milton and Rose Friedman and Friedrich von Hayek.

Of course, neoliberalism is based on the very strong assumption that people's preferences—preferences that determine what they consume and how much they strive to become rich—are simply a given and not the subject of social control or manipulation by others. If this assumption does not hold, then the behaviour of consumers reflects not their own preferences but the preferences of the organisations and institutions that influence them. Even the most ardent neoliberal must admit exceptions to the rule. It is conceded that children should not be permitted to choose to eat only fast food, spend their inheritance, or inject themselves with heroin. But, as long as they remain sane, once children reach their majority they are taken to be fully conscious of their interests and wholly responsible for any decisions that turn out to be contrary to their interests. Any decision they make, as long as it does not impinge on the rights of others, is deemed to be beyond reproach.[2] However, as the exceptions already begin to suggest, an analysis of the structure, meaning and political implications of consumption behaviour demonstrates that the idea of consumer sovereignty is very shallow.

Economics goes further than maintaining that the consumption choices of individuals are sacrosanct by defending the benefits of choice itself. It argues that an extension of the range of choices available to consumers in itself improves wellbeing because it enables each consumer to match more nearly their consumption spending to their wants. One immediate problem here is that the idea covers only one type of choice, the choice between different goods for sale. It excludes the possibility that consumers may prefer to limit the choices available to them— because, for example, it is too hard to choose from too great a variety or because they have a moral objection to some of the choices on offer. It also excludes the preference of some consumers to live in a society free of a vast array of trivially differentiated products, pervasive advertising, and unrelenting attempts to persuade them that their consumption choices can make them happy.

The more important fault in the argument, however, is the assumption that consumers come to the market with their wants already determined, and the only question is how best to satisfy them from the range of goods and services available. It is perverse to characterise the market as a want-satisfying mechanism when we are exposed every day to attempts by the market to influence what we want. Consumers' preferences do not develop 'outside the system'; they are created and reinforced by the system, so that consumer *sovereignty* is a myth. The question is not one of personal consumer choice versus elitist social engineering; it is one of corporate manipulation of consumer behaviour versus individuals in society understanding what is in their real interests. For most people this is an obvious point, but, as we will see, its implications are far-reaching. The issue goes well beyond the role of advertisers in shaping consumer preferences and purchasing behaviour: we must consider the social and psychological milieu of consumer society that teaches people how to think about themselves and their goals. The influence of the marketing society actually undermines the foundations of philosophical liberalism because, instead of society being populated by free agents rationally maximising their welfare through their consumption choices, it is peopled by complex beings whose tastes, priorities and value systems are, to a large degree, manipulated by the very 'markets' that are supposed to serve them.

One of the ironies of the modern world is that choice has been elevated to supreme status precisely at a time of social and cultural homogenisation across the globe. Henry Ford famously said of his automobiles that customers could choose any colour they liked so long as it was black. Today we are told that we can choose any goods we like so long as they meet the norms of US consumer culture. The 'choice' of the economics texts and the neoliberal political philosophers is not true choice: it is manufactured variety. Rather than providing a range of possibilities tailored to meet individual needs, the variety of products serves to confuse consumers, not only about what will satisfy their wants but also about what their wants actually are.[3]

Consumption and the modern self

While economics imagines that consumption of goods is a straightforward process of satisfying human wants or desires, in fact people's relationship with their possessions is full of psychological complexity. Objects are not just useful: they have meaning. We do not have difficulty recognising this with certain objects in some cultural contexts. It is a cliche to observe that for men cars are often 'power objects', symbols of virility, strength, achievement and coolness, and that they may use cars to project this image to compensate for feelings of inadequacy. Economics is stuck in a pre-consumerist belief that people buy goods to satisfy basic human needs, but modern consumers no longer consume the 'utility' of goods and services: they consume their symbolic meanings. It is almost impossible today to buy any item that its producer has not attempted to invest with symbolic meaning. Clothing, for example, is designed to send signals. Even underwear that might be seen by no one is bought and sold because it makes the wearer feel a certain way about themselves. It can be sexy, sensible, muscular, vibrant, suave or whimsical and can communicate a variety of sexual connotations—demure but willing, titillating, brazen, romantic or naughty. The signals it is designed to send are the subject of meticulous commercial calculation.

In pre-industrial societies, a range of physical objects communicated status and power—shells, penis gourds, feathers, orbs, jewellery, and so on. In modern consumer society the essential symbol of status has taken the most abstract form, the form of money. The social function of the power of money was particularly apparent to chroniclers of society in the period of transition from feudalism to capitalism. Karl Marx was one of the most astute observers of the change. In his *Economic and Philosophic*

Manuscripts of 1844 he wrote of the power of money in the new society in the following terms:

> The extent of the power of money is my power. Money's properties are my properties and essential powers—the properties and powers of its possessor . . . I am bad, dishonest, unscrupulous, stupid; but money is honoured, and therefore so is its possessor. Money is the supreme good, therefore its possessor is good. Money, besides, saves me the trouble of being dishonest: I am therefore presumed honest.

But even before the emergence of industrial society the transformative power of money was a common theme. In *Timon of Athens* Shakespeare wrote:

> Gold? Yellow, glittering, precious gold? . . . Thus much of this will make black white, foul fair,
> Wrong right, base noble, old young, coward valiant.

In one study of the relationship between people and their possessions, the researchers used psychological measures to categorise families' homes as 'warm' or 'cool', depending on the strength of 'emotional integration' within the family. They found that people from warm homes are much less attached to the objects in their homes and, where objects do have value, their worth depends on the meaning they carry as signs of relationships between people. People from cool homes are much less likely to talk of the emotional significance of objects for their relationships, and indeed often dislike being questioned about their possessions, claiming that people are more important than things:

This rejection of the symbolic mediation of things in favor of direct human ties seemed plausible at first, until we began to notice that people who denied meanings to objects also lacked any close network of human relationships. Those who were most vocal about prizing friendship over material concerns seemed to be the most lonely and isolated.[4]

Psychologists have confirmed the relationship between family structure and consumption behaviour. One study showed that young adults who had been reared in disrupted families are more materialistic and display higher levels of compulsive consumption than young adults reared in intact families.[5] Compulsive consumption may be a coping strategy, in which material goods compensate for the relative absence of emotional warmth.

The authors of the 'warm homes, cool homes' study ask what explains the modern addiction to material things: 'A great deal of the energy we consume goes to providing comfort: more and more elaborate houses, clothes, food, and gadgets. The energy we use still serves ends that mimic basic needs—food, warmth, security, and so on—but have now become addictive habits rather than necessities'.[6] This, of course, is in sharp contrast to the official story promoted by neoliberal economists, in which goods are the bearers of 'utility', objects that simply satisfy human needs. While we are increasingly dependent on the market economy, the nature of our lives makes it more difficult for us to express our identity and be acknowledged for who we are. This engenders a sense of impotence, an unheard cry for recognition from the 'joyless consumer', so that material possessions serve as 'pacifiers for the self-induced helplessness we have created'.[7] Consumption becomes an emotional habit in which the consumer is repeatedly trying to restore the tenuous bonds of self. When this is understood, the idea that people acquire goods to satisfy their material needs becomes a parody of itself.

For people without wealth in pre-industrial society, personal identity was derived from their daily activities, from their occupations. Family names such as Smith, Fletcher, Farmer and Cutler remind us of this. Today this is no longer true: in consumer society people attempt to create an identity not from what they produce but from what they consume. People were once comfortable deriving their identities from their productive activity, but people today must hide the fact that they manufacture their selves from what they consume. We do not expect that people will take to naming themselves 'John Sports Utility' or 'Barbara Georgian Mansion', yet in consumer society we behave in ways that are only marginally less obtuse. In the words of one of the world's largest producers of consumer products:

> . . . the brand defines the consumer. We are what we wear, what we eat, what we drive. Each of us in this room is a walking compendium of brands. The collection of brands we choose to assemble around us have become amongst the most direct expressions of our individuality—or more precisely, our deep psychological need to identify ourselves with others.[8]

While we tend to think of the pursuit of status as the preoccupation of the wealthy, the poor may be just as smitten. Consider young urban African-Americans in the United States who have created an industry aimed at projecting a certain image of laid-back coolness with a hint of menace.

Advertisers understand the power of this. A few years ago, the marketing experts at Cadbury decided to reposition for the teenage market the children's lollipop sold as Chupa Chups. Recognising that teenagers resist being advertised to, Cadbury produced a series of abstract television commercials that were irreverent and striking.[9] The campaign has been phenomenally successful. But sales of Chupa Chups—the name means 'suck a lot' in Spanish—have boomed largely because of the product's association with drug use. Teenagers taking amphetamines and ecstasy, especially at rave parties, suck the lollipop to stop themselves from grinding their teeth and biting the inside of their mouth. Some rave venues sell Chupa Chups as an essential accessory. In teenage culture, the product has now become associated with non-conformity and having a good time outside the law. This 'bad' image is a priceless marketing asset that gives the product credibility in the teenage market, one that spills over into everyday purchases by those who simply associate it with being cool, that hard-to-define personal characteristic that is essential to successfully navigating teenage years.

Market ideology asserts that free choice allows consumers to express their 'individuality'. Extending the essence of liberalism, libertarian political philosophy counterposes the freedoms of the individual against those of the collective, and especially the state. Consumer capitalism trades on the modern desire for individuality, to mark oneself out from the crowd. However, as the sociologist George Simmel told us many years ago, the individuality of modern urban life is a pseudo-individuality of exaggerated behaviours and contrived attitudes. The individuality of the marketing society is an elaborate pose people adopt to cover up the fact that they have been buried in the homogenising forces of consumer culture. The consumer self is garishly differentiated on the outside, but this differentiation serves only to conceal the dull conformity of the inner self.

In fact, to discover true individuality it is necessary to stage a psychological withdrawal from the market economy, since that is a place where one can buy only manufactured identities—masks bought to provide clones with the appearance of difference. The market is a place where compulsive differentiation becomes a substitute for the individual. For some people, an inability or unwillingness to meet the demands of manufactured identity becomes too much to bear. Reaction against pseudo-individuality can sometimes take extreme forms, such as escape into cults that control and crush the true individual by different means.

Nowhere has the existential ennui of consumption been more apparent than in Japan, where the search for some sense of reality and authentic selfhood intensified as the decades of economic success passed, until finally it was engulfed by the economic malaise and political soul-searching of the 1990s. As Gavan McCormack, one of the sharpest Japan watchers, observes, in the early 1990s Japan had reached the pinnacle of growth—vastly outstripping the income of all other Asian countries, exceeding the United States in income per person, with no unemployment, boasting the world's nine biggest banks, and funding the current account deficits of countries around the world. Japan was on track to become the world's biggest economy 'thus matching, and exceeding, the highest ambitions, and the wildest dreams, of not only the preceding fifty years but of the century and a half since Japan began to pursue the path of Westernization and modernization'.[10] According to some of the more percipient Japanese observers, though, after this fantastic success Japanese society has been left with an emptiness that no amount of consumer goods can fill and a nagging question that bedevils public discourse: What have we sacrificed to have the world's nine biggest banks?

In the 1980s Japan's search for something beyond work and consumption centred on the development of theme parks, with Tokyo Disneyland, founded in 1983, proving enormously successful. These diverting endeavours have been attacked by Japanese critics as attempts to create a 'hyper-reality' to escape from the anxieties and stresses of ordinary life. McCormack paraphrases one critic's scathing analysis of Tokyo Disneyland, 'a central cultural symbol of the new Japan':

> This 'Happiest Place on Earth', which is gradually being replicated in the shopping malls and exhibition centers of the 1990s, allows visitors to consume the prepackaged American symbols of fantasy, love, and adventure passively, while depriving them of opportunities for spontaneous festivity and human interaction.[11]

In this infantile world, adults escape into a make-believe land whose predominant characteristic is 'cuteness', as if the pointlessness of adult life can be forgotten through a reversion to childishness.

The pseudo-individuality of modern consumer culture is isolating. The more isolated we are, the more we are preoccupied with what other people think of us and the more inclined we are to manufacture an identity to project onto the world. The dramatic increase in the incidence of depression in the last few decades seems to be directly associated with loss of social networks and personal closeness, which in turn are the products of mobility and the substitution of shopping and commercial entertainment for community-based activity. According to Robert Lane, 'Three factors contribute to social isolation within market economies: television viewing, the shopping experience and the nature of what is consumed'.[12]

When a terrorist attack caused the twin towers of the World Trade Center to collapse on 11 September 2001, killing almost 3000 people, within days President Bush was telling the American public that the best way they could show that they would not be cowed by terrorism was to go out and shop. Although this was partly a response to fears that a collapse in consumer confidence would prompt a prolonged recession, the advice was presented as a means by which Americans could demonstrate their defiance. Consumer spending was characterised as a 'patriotic duty' for those who wanted to demonstrate that America would not be diverted from its way of life. In other words, the most normal act in the United States is to consume. The presidential blessing of shopping helped 'to counteract the worries, the gloom, the feelings of guilt aroused by shopping in a time of trauma'. The guilt associated with shopping is an acknowledgment of the selfishness and triviality of the act. Evoking the well-worn words of a previous president, PBS reporter Paul Solman concluded, 'Shopping may not only be what you can do for your country, but . . . what you can do for yourself as well'.[13]

After September 11, shopping was the drug administered to heal the nation's wounds, a process of collective retail therapy that revealed the profound psychological and social importance of the act of consumption. Although aware of it only subliminally, President Bush was quite right to understand that the myriad acts of everyday consumer spending are inseparable from the ideological reproduction of consumer capitalism.

We know that depression is an increasingly common experience for people in Western societies. It is often associated with a feeling of meaninglessness, a niggling sense that there is no point. Such a feeling is often embarrassing to admit to in a social milieu where life is supposed to be an endless round of good times, and this silence does much to explain the horrifying rise in youth suicide. A common response to this existential depression is to go shopping. Shopping, especially for items other than daily necessities, has a range of powerful associations that have seeped into our consciousnesses. We are subtly schooled to feel that to possess is to capture power; indeed, that possessions are the source of power in our society. A subconscious association tells us that if we have power over goods we will have power over life— at least over our own lives.

If shopping has become the activity through which we try to give meaning to our lives, the shopping malls that now embellish every city are the shrines we build to this power. Ostensibly, shopping malls are no more than a convenient way to gain access to a variety of services. But there is a powerful and carefully manufactured psychology to the shopping mall. Unlike the traditional market, the bazaar or even the suburban high street, shopping malls are devoted exclusively to consumer activity—to spending money. The shopping mall feels quite different from the world outside. We enter a trance-like state when we enter one, a sort of meditation in which the mantra that focuses our attention is the promise of acquisition. The mall provides insulation against a hostile world. In a perverse way, shopping malls are liberating; we feel that all those goods, all that power, are there for us.

One powerful confirmation of this psychological function of the act of purchasing is the attitude we adopt to goods that we have acquired free of charge. Somehow we have less regard for freely given goods than for goods we have acquired through spending our own money. When we spend our own money we feel we are investing part of ourselves in what we buy, so that we can spread the power of our egos beyond the confines of our bodies. The devaluation of free goods is often overridden by other cultural norms or feelings, such as the satisfaction derived from eating something grown in a home garden. But in children it is quite apparent. Modern children crave things that have been bought in a shop. Meals cooked at home, clothes sewn at home and toys made at home lack the magic of consumption. Children learn that a thing they have saved their own money to buy or a thing for which their parents have 'sacrificed' their money has enormous value; it gives them a taste of the personal power conferred by purchasing power.

The shopping mall has none of the communal functions of the marketplace; its sole function is to sell, and in so doing it strives to give meaning to alienated lives. Contradictory as it may seem, shopping is an attempt to recapture a sense of community. Fox and Lears trace the changes in the social functions of consumption:

Life for most middle-class and many working-class
Americans in the twentieth century has been a ceaseless
pursuit of the 'good life' and a constant reminder of their
powerlessness . . . Although the dominant institutions of
our culture have purported to be offering the consumer a
fulfilling participation in the life of the community, they
have to a large extent presented the empty prospect of
taking part in the marketplace of personal exchange.[14]

People naturally pursue a sense of community and belonging.
With the breakdown of old communities and the emergence of
the economic individual under industrial capitalism, the new
sense of society embraced whole countries rather than local
communities. People began to perceive that the path to accept-
ability in the new society was to adopt, as always, the socially
appropriate forms of behaviour. These new forms of behaviour
stressed income and material acquisition. Since everyone seemed
to want this above all, acquisitiveness became the means of
finding a sense of community. But what a solitary sense of
community it turned out to be! It was to be had not by interacting
with other people but by purchasing disembodied, impersonal
products in the marketplace—as if by purchasing socially
sanctioned goods we could buy a sense of belonging. Ignoring
those around us, we came to look for a sense of community on
the shelves of the supermarkets and the clothing stores.

Shopping is a response to our existential depression, when
the world seems to overwhelm us, when we feel we have been put
on Earth only to drag ourselves through a life of drudgery.
Fleetingly, we can break out and rebel by going shopping.

Shopping is even tinged by a sense of challenge to the world, to the lives we are stuck in; it is a rebuke to the system that tries to engulf us. 'I can't afford it but, damn it, I'll buy it anyway.' Ultimately, though, shopping can be no release; it can only enmesh us further. The fleeting sense of power that comes with a purchase simply leaves a greater void to be filled. It is like struggling to get out of quicksand—by struggling, we just sink deeper into the mire. In the end, to consume is to concede defeat; to consume like this is to slowly die.

The cry for riches to fill the existential void is not of course a wholly modern phenomenon. For centuries it has been understood that the hope invested in material wealth can only turn into greater hope, leaving happiness a dream. Goethe knew:

> Blundering with desire towards fruition,
> And in fruition pining for desire.[15]

But, whereas this futile activity was reserved for the few in previous ages, today it is the province of the mass of ordinary people. While the personal evidence of the futility of material acquisitiveness mounts, we continue to be assailed everywhere, every day of our lives, by messages that affirm the power of money. The power of money is true enough: people with money are powerful in Western society. But they are only powerful in the particular sense of having control over material resources and over other people. Those who are driven to ever greater accumulation of things are driven by inner urges and unmet needs that they neither understand nor control.

Consumption today is marketed as a means of participating in society. Telephone services, telecommunications and the

Internet are promoted as means by which people can keep in touch with the world. But, as E.J. Mishan remarked in the 1960s, with all the enormous advances in communications, people know less of their neighbours than ever before in human history.[16] The absence of real contact induces desperate attempts to fill the silence with trivial noise and distractions—the muzak of the malls, commercial radio, and televisions in airport lounges.[17] This unease with silence and stillness is a modern phenomenon, but it has been developing at least since the time of rapid urbanisation. John Stuart Mill was one of the first to notice the psychological impact of increased population density and the urbanisation of society: 'It is not good for a man to be kept perforce at all times in the presence of his species. A world from which solitude is extirpated is a very poor ideal. Solitude, in the sense of being often alone, is essential to any depth of meditation or of character'.[18]

One might say that this is the affliction of our age—too much loneliness and not enough solitude.

Marketing

Modern consumer capitalism will flourish as long as what people desire outpaces what they have. It is thus vital to the reproduction of the system that individuals are constantly made to feel dissatisfied with what they have. The irony of this should not be missed: while economic growth is said to be the process whereby people's wants are satisfied so that they become happier—and economics is defined as the study of how scarce resources are best used to maximise welfare—in reality economic growth can be sustained only as long as people remain discontented. Economic growth does not create happiness: unhappiness sustains economic growth. Thus discontent must be continually fomented if modern consumer capitalism is to survive. This explains the indispensable role of the advertising industry.

Economic ideology contends that consumers with pre-existing preferences come to the market to choose from what is available. In reality, the advertising industry exists because the reverse is true. Most frequently, corporations manufacture a product, usually just a variation on an existing product, and then set about creating a market for it. Innocent of the economics texts, the marketing experts know there are no consumer products today that are bought solely for their usefulness. They are all purchased for the contribution they are expected to make to the consumer's self-image or lifestyle, whether it be a 'new' design for jeans, a repackaged tub of margarine, an exciting new financial product, or a car that may or may not perform better but will undoubtedly make the owner feel more potent, laid back, liberated or worldly.

The greatest danger to consumer capitalism is the possibility that people in wealthy countries will decide that they have more or less everything they need. For each individual this is a small realisation, but it has momentous social implications. For an increasingly jaded population, deceived for decades into believing that the way to a contented life is material acquisition, the task of the advertising industry becomes ever more challenging. As a result, a large portion of the creative energy of wealthy nations is channelled into the marketing machine, leaving us to speculate on the truly enriching cultural outpouring that would be possible if this energy were devoted to more productive ends.

Advertising long ago discarded the practice of selling a product on the merits of its useful features. Modern marketing builds symbolic associations between the product and the psychological states of potential consumers, sometimes targeting known feelings of inadequacy, aspiration or expectation and sometimes setting out to create a sense of inadequacy in order to remedy it with the product. On the face of it, a kitchen-cleaning product is promoted for its ability to clean, but in reality it is sold because it provides the customer with the sense of being a devoted home-maker or because a single person is reminded of how it was at home. If this fails to generate enough sales, an advertisement can create anxiety in people by suggesting that their kitchen is seething with 'hidden germs' that could at any time infect their children. Most four-wheel-drive vehicles never leave the city: they are sold to people who want to create for themselves and others the image that they are outgoing, adventurous types, able to cast off the shackles of urban living and 'rough it' with nature. Increasing numbers of people pay large sums to live out this fantasy, despite the well-established environmental damage and accident mortality rates associated with four-wheel-drive vehicles.

So much is obvious. Other products are targeted at particular groups, to take advantage of and reinforce their distinctness— 'platinum' credit cards, to make people at the top end of the market feel special about themselves; outdoor clothes, for people who think they are rebelling against consumerism; city runabouts, for young adults with a need to be seen to be having fun. To acquire a place in the social structure, each person must express a particular set of values. Money gives more options for expressing a desired set of values, but it is not essential. Expressing a set of values shows others who you see yourself to be. The art of the successful modern consumer is to consume in a way that says 'this is who I am' without it being apparent that the statement is being made. So we snigger at those who declare themselves too blatantly, the innocent consumers who expose the system by not understanding the rules.

When consumers are at the point of making a purchase they are subliminally asking themselves two questions: Who am I? Who do I want to be? These questions of meaning and identity are the most profound questions humans can pose, yet today they are expressed in the lines of a car and shape of a soft-drink bottle. The advertising industry demands such creativity of its employees because the creeping sense of failure associated with consumption requires continual invention of new ways of appealing to the need for personal identity.

Thus the task of the advertising industry is to uncover the complex set of feelings associated with particular products and to design marketing campaigns to appeal to those feelings. This is a challenge: consumers, for the most part, do not consciously understand what they want or why they want it. One of the newer techniques to elicit information is known as 'metaphor marketing'.[19] Developed by Harvard polymath Jerry Zaltman, the technique is based on the recognition that, while most market research relies on words, human beings think in and react to visual images. Metaphor marketing asks potential consumers to select from magazines and other media images that, for whatever reason, they associate with certain products. The rationale is encapsulated in a quote, used by Zaltman, from the surrealist painter René Magritte: 'Everything we see hides something else we want to see'.

Subsequent reflection on and interpretation of the images selected by the potential consumers reveal unexpected associations and desires. For example, women hate wearing panty hose because they are hot and uncomfortable in summer. But reflection on the pictures women associate with panty hose reveals that they also like wearing them because they make them feel thin and tall and therefore alluring. A Nestlé candy bar was found to have the expected associations with a quick snack, but analysis of the images consumers picked out showed that the candy bar is also a powerful icon of time, one that evokes images of a simpler era of childhood. When researchers investigated the metaphors associated with a new home-security system they were surprised to discover how often consumers chose images of dogs, which for the interviewers symbolise comfort and security. Instead of the device being marketed as a high-tech electronic system, dogs provide a powerful image that evokes the feelings that persuade consumers to buy security systems.

Prodigious intellectual and creative effort is poured into marketing, driven by the imperative of consumer capitalism. All aspects of human psychology—our fears, our sources of shame, our sexuality, our spiritual yearnings—are a treasure house to be plundered in the search for a commercial edge. Thousands of the most creative individuals in modern society, such as Zaltman and his colleagues, devote their lives to helping corporations manipulate people into buying more of their brand of margarine or running shoes at the expense of another corporation selling a virtually identical product. This is not just a waste of talent. The work of Zaltman and many like him is at best meaningless and at worst a subtle form of cultural brainwashing whose purpose is to sustain a system that leaves people miserable. This fact is widely understood but elicits no condemnation. It is regarded as normal.

The sophistication and subtlety of some advertising campaigns should not be underestimated. A television advertisement for a brand of margarine takes the viewer through a series of carefully constructed images designed to evoke a particular mood. Backed by an evocative song, the advertisement tells the story of a modern working mother, a nurse returning home from work through the bustle of the city to the arms of her four-year-old daughter. Shot through orange filters to give a sense of warmth and closeness, mother and daughter talk while mother prepares a meal in the kitchen. The child makes a phone call to her daddy, who we see works on an oil rig somewhere out in the ocean. Each camera shot evokes the sense of an intimate, loving family temporarily separated and longing to be reunited. The woman takes the phone and talks to her man. She is stoic in his absence; he is a new man, masculine but soft and loving, and there is a hint of the sexual in their expressions. We know this adoring family will be reunited in their home and all will be right with the world. The purpose of the commercial is to leave the viewer with a set of associations between the ideal family and this brand of margarine.

In the marketing of margarine, the product's contribution to the wellbeing of the consumer is wholly divorced from any of its physical properties. The actual usefulness of the product has become irrelevant, so that the consumer does not buy something to spread on bread but a concatenation of feelings associated with idealised family relationships. The complex, clever symbolism of the advertisement is designed to convince the viewer that a tub of vegetable fat that is identical to half a dozen other brands of vegetable fat can give us something very special, something we really need. A moment's reflection by even the most gullible consumer reveals the absurdity of this, but the strategy works because it is built on two facets of human psychology. In a world of social disintegration, modern consumers have a powerful need for family warmth, and humans, just like Pavlov's dogs, make unconscious associations. Unmet emotional needs and unconscious association are the twin psychological pillars of the marketing society.

However, some forms of marketing have now entered a new phase that no longer targets specific emotional needs. In the last fifteen or so years corporations have taken marketing beyond the particular product by creating an entire culture associated with their brand; the product itself needs only to have features that are consistent with the lifestyle or attitude the brand represents. Naomi Klein argues in *No Logo* that, 'Rather than serving as a guarantee of value on a product, the brand itself has increasingly become the product, a free-standing idea pasted onto innumerable surfaces. The actual product bearing the brand-name has become a medium, like radio or a billboard, to transmit the real message'.[20] The product itself is incidental to the company and indeed in many cases its manufacture is contracted out to factories in the Third World. Klein refers to this as a 'race towards weightlessness', in which the company distances itself from the manufacture of a product and becomes a shell devoted to marketing. In the world of the weightless corporation, the real work is to build a brand rather than make a product. This represents a shift from the product itself being of true value: what is of true value is 'the idea, the lifestyle, the attitude', and it is these associations with a product that require the real investment and creativity.

The expense associated with creating and sustaining a brand, including advertising and sponsorships, explains the cavernous gap between what it costs to actually manufacture a pair of shoes, for example, and the price the consumer pays. The consumer is paying for an attitude as well as for footwear, and most of the money is spent on attempting to invest the shoes with attitude. This sophisticated process involves the modification of culture; Klein describes it as the 'cultural looting of public and mental spaces':

> Power, for a brand-driven company, is attained not by collecting assets per se, but by projecting one's brand idea onto as many surfaces of the culture as possible: the wall of a college, a billboard the size of a skyscraper, an ad campaign that waxes philosophic about the humane future of our global village.

While traditional marketing is aimed at creating associations between a product and personal attributes, branding goes beyond association: 'The goal now is for the brands to animate their marketing identities, to become real world living manifestations of their myths. Brands are about "meaning", not product attributes'.

The search for a marketing edge has meant the colonisation of all cultural forms. Even the opposition to this cultural looting represented by the anti-globalisation movement, for which *No Logo* has become an iconic text, is now exploited. Italian clothing company Diesel advertises directly to the anti-globalisation demographic, even going so far as to describe its brand as a 'movement', with images of Diesel-clad protesters dressed in a post-punk Euro-alternative style. The images—with the Diesel logo discreetly placed because this group reacts badly to being advertised at—are targeted at customers aged 20 to 29 who are so cool that being cool does not matter any more. The 'no logo' generation itself, whose ironic attitude to popular culture separates it from the teenage market, has become the latest cultural mine for marketers.

The beauty of this approach is that consumers can never get what they want. Products and brands can never give real meaning to human lives, so modern consumers lapse into a permanent state of unfulfilled desire. This, of course, is the essential state for consumers in modern capitalism. Reversing the traditional process of first developing a product and then considering how best to market it, it is not uncommon today for a corporation to come up with an idea for a promotion before the product itself is developed. The product is then designed to fit the idea. In the case of the marketing of pop groups, the music can be written, sometimes electronically, so that it appeals to a predetermined demographic with certain cultural aspirations; the songs are recorded by session musicians, and only later are the members of the band chosen and made over to fit the planned image.

There is, however, a fragility built into the structure of branding. For marketing that focuses on a product, when the

product has a problem it simply fails as a product and the corporation that made it can move on; the Ford Edsel is often used as
an example of an expensive flop. But when Nike's use of
sweatshops in Indonesia is exposed, when McDonald's is accused
of destroying Amazon rain forests and exploiting its teenage
workers, and when Shell is shown to be associated with state-
sanctioned murder in Nigeria there is no escape. As Klein points
out, 'Many of the people who inhabit these branded worlds feel
complicit in their wrongs, both guilty and connected. And this
connection is a volatile one, akin to the relationship of fan and
celebrity: emotionally intense but shallow enough to turn on a
dime'.[21] This fragility provides a target for activists: the creation
of a brand image invites iconoclasm, and this has spawned a new
method of resistance known as 'culture jamming'.[22]

Contrary to the fiction of the economics texts, in which independent consumers go in search of the products that will satisfy
their needs, humans have become extensions of the products they
consume. When people assume manufactured identities, instead
of searching for their real selves, they come together as collectiv-
ities of attitudes and elaborate poses rather than real flesh and
blood, and this has profound implications for the nature of social
interaction.

What is it that has turned consumers of products into
consumers of lifestyle and seekers of attitude? The answer is clear:
it is the emptiness of modern life that leads people on a vain search
for the thing that will fill the void. It is a need to create an identity, as much to know oneself as to have something to project onto
the world, in a society in which the growth fetish has trivialised,
marginalised or destroyed many of the things that truly can

provide fulfilment. What is the impact of the tyranny of brands on those whose lives are governed by them—gullible consumers—which must include almost everyone in Western societies? It is to reinforce the insidious sense that something is missing, to create the conditions for serial disappointment, yet to sustain hope that more of what has so far failed will ultimately succeed.

The advertising industry is the primary agent of this massive deception. To protect itself it hides behind an elaborate facade. The official story is that advertising helps discerning consumers make informed choices about how best to spend their money. This ideology of consumer sovereignty is used to establish and maintain a taboo. We are not allowed to point out that advertising, and the pervasive commercialism of everyday life, influences ordinary citizens to behave in ways that are contrary to their interests. The fiction is maintained in advertising codes of practice that verge on the laughable. As in other wealthy countries, in Britain the Code of Advertising Standards and Practice declares, 'No advertisement may contain any descriptions, claims or illustrations which expressly or by implication mislead'. In particular, 'No advertisement may misleadingly claim or imply that the product advertised, or an ingredient, has some special property or quality that is incapable of being established'. If governments were serious about this criterion of ethical behaviour, the advertising industry would effectively be abolished. For is not the purpose of advertising to give people the impression that the product has some special property or quality that is in fact entirely unrelated to the product itself? Do not advertisers attempt to persuade us that cars can give us sexual potency or express our level of achievement, that a detergent can allow a woman to demonstrate that she is a loving mother, that those who buy a particular brand of margarine can create happy and loving families, that a certain brand of beer confers hard-working manhood, that a leather briefcase can provide a sense of power in the world of business, and so on ad infinitum? These claims are all blatantly and demonstrably misleading. The Code of Advertising Standards and Practice goes on to assert that advertisements 'must not seek to exploit public ignorance or to perpetuate popular misconceptions'. Apart from the specific popular misconceptions associated with, for example, ownership of a Ferrari or wearing Diesel jeans, the social function of advertising is precisely to perpetuate the popular misconception that life satisfaction can be increased by way of consumption of material goods.

The United States has similar provisions guarding the consumer against 'misleading and deceptive' advertising, despite the fact that it is hard to find any advertisement that is not grossly misleading as to the effects of the product and that is explicitly designed to deceive. Indeed, an advertising agency that failed to mislead potential consumers into believing that they could derive enhanced personal qualities from a product would not be in business for long. US law appears to have an escape clause for the industry: an act must not mislead the 'reasonable consumer', and an advertiser is not liable for 'every conceivable misconception, however outlandish, to which his representations may be subject among the foolish or feeble-minded'.[23] It would not occur to the legislators, regulators and jurists who might be called on to make a judgment that today's average consumer may be an everyday victim of foolishness and feeble-mindedness in their consumption behaviour.

Any reasonable assessment must conclude that the vast majority of advertising 'exploits public ignorance and perpetuates misconceptions'. It is deliberately designed to mislead the reasonable consumer, so should be banned. Moreover, given that the bulk of advertising aims to persuade consumers to change from one brand to another where the material differences between the brands are minimal, the resource savings would be enormous if advertising were banned. The resources that are currently eaten up in a zero-sum game could be devoted to spending that could make a large contribution to human well-being—through, for example, public health programs in the Third World. In addition, banning advertising would begin the process of undoing the association between material consumption and happiness, an association that, because it is untrue, causes so much personal disappointment. One result would be that over time people would simply consume less, a process that must begin sooner rather than later if there is to be any hope of sustaining the material basis of human existence on Earth. By persuading people to buy more and more, advertising promotes continued degradation of the environment. While governments exhort their citizens to protect the environment through the slogan 'reduce, re-use and recycle', a huge advertising industry persuades people to 'increase, discard and dump'. Needless to say, this is a very unequal battle, particularly because it is a matter of life or death for the corporations, whereas, for most governments, urging people to 'do the right thing' is little more than a cheap sop to voter concern about the parlous state of the environment.

Returning to Chapter 2's discussion of the meaning of wellbeing, we are reminded that deeper states of contentment are associated with states of psychological maturation and self-actualisation, or individuation, in which unconscious drives and motivations are brought to consciousness and, through a process of psychological integration, harmonised with one's conscious goals and principles. Thus advertising will continue to be effective as long as people are driven by unconscious desires and motivations, but it begins to fail for those who have reached a more advanced state of self-awareness. In other words, advertising promises things to make people happy, so it works only as long as people are unhappy. When people reach a state of integration, they can stage a psychological withdrawal from the market and begin to create themselves just as they please.

Overconsumption

Nutritionists describe obesity in terms of energy imbalance, usually caused by excessive calorie consumption and insufficient physical activity. In a previous era it might have been described, perhaps more usefully, in terms of gluttony and sloth.[24] As with other excesses, promotion of gluttony—a form of overconsumption that directly affects the body—is a product of consumer society. Food manufacturers compete fiercely to win market share by engineering foods that appeal to the palate. The result is that most of the foods offered today in supermarkets and fast-food outlets are laced with fat, sugar and salt. This fierce competition does not simply persuade consumers to change from one product to another: it also means that consumers eat more. Sixty-one per cent of American adults are now overweight (defined as having a body mass index over 25) or obese (body mass index over 30); 14 per cent of adolescents are in the same category. This is a new phenomenon. The prevalence of obesity among adolescents has trebled in the past two decades.[25] As with many other aspects of social change, the United States leads the way, showing the future of the rest of the industrialised world.

Although genetic and metabolic factors play a role, the principal causes of the spread of obesity are behavioural and socio-cultural.[26] Some people are better able to resist the temptations offered by food manufacturers. The overwhelming majority of obese people overeat for psychological reasons, just as other people indulge in overconsumption of cars, clothes and houses for psychological reasons. The so-called epidemic of obesity has occurred only in the last twenty or, at most, thirty years. Yet, as with other addictions and social pathologies (including ADD), it is safer to medicalise the problem and thus refer to it as an 'epidemic'. The North American Association for the Study of Obesity insists that 'we must begin to view obesity as a medical problem'.[27] Of course, medical problems are ones sorted out between patient and doctor and are best cured by drugs and surgery, especially drugs, so that the pharmaceutical industry can expand to undo the effects of the food industry. (One of the primary demands of the obesity lobby is for obesity to be given formal medical status so that health insurance companies are required to pay for treatment.) Both the pharmaceutical and the food industries profit from obesity and, once again, the medical profession and drug companies play a crucial role in diverting us from asking what it is about our society that gives rise to these pathologies.

The medical profession thus helps to validate overconsumption. According to the authors of an article in the *British Medical Journal*:

> . . . the driving force for the increasing prevalence of obesity in populations is the increasingly obesogenic environment rather than any 'pathology' in metabolic defects or genetic mutations within individuals. A paradigm shift to understanding obesity as 'normal physiology within a pathological environment' signposts the directions for a wider public health approach to the obesity problem.[28]

This is a striking notion. Obese people may be thought of as behaving normally in a sick social environment, although characterising obesity as a public health problem should not conceal the fact that it is in reality a social pathology that spills over into health problems. Like all species, humans instinctively conserve energy, expending just what they need to feed and breed. Our instinct is to minimise activity, something the modern sedentary lifestyle in rich countries permits as never before. Obesity, then, is an environmental health problem reflecting both the range of food choices available and the opportunity to reduce physical activity. Medical solutions to obesity will not work because they fail to tackle the causes. Prevention requires wholesale change in the culture of consumption, which itself is a reaction to the emptiness of affluence. This is not meant as an attack on people who have succumbed to obesity; they, after all, are the victims. Yet overweight people are often vilified; not, one suspects, for being too weak to resist temptation, but for revealing in such a confronting way our dirty secret of overconsumption.

We have stressed that consumption no longer occurs in order to meet human needs; its purpose now is to manufacture identity. The nature of consumption spending has changed from an activity aimed at acquiring status through displays of wealth to one of creating the self through association with certain products and brands. We no longer want to keep up with the Joneses; we want to trump the Joneses by differentiating ourselves from them. The transformation of useful goods into lifestyle accessories has implications for production as well as consumption. In order for goods to serve as the accoutrements of lifestyle they must have additional qualities built into them, and the extra costs form part of their value. These extra costs are partly those of product differentiation and partly those of creating and renewing the image and the brand. Almost all consumer goods now have luxurious or stylistic aspects built into them that inflate their prices. This price inflation sometimes raises the cost of a product several times beyond the level required to make an item that satisfies some reasonable need for sustenance, shelter, clothing, education or entertainment. Watches that sell for $2000, sunglasses with $700 price tags, running shoes and shirts that cost $200, highly engineered and luxuriously appointed cars for $50 000 and more, houses with double the necessary floor space—all these have features that are redundant and some have features that are undetectable even to the consumer. A fake Rolex is indistinguishable from a genuine one, except that the wearer knows he is only pretending to be the person he wants to pretend to be. Next to a photo of a stylish young mother with a smiling baby on her back, a magazine advertises 'what every mother and baby wants for their afternoon stroll', a chinchilla baby backpack selling for $12 000 (plus a matching chinchilla collar and cuffs for mother, priced at $4995).

This value-inflation process is essential, since in its absence consumers would be unable to spend the incomes that have resulted from decades of sustained economic growth. In other words, in those parts of the world where most people have everything they could reasonably want in order to satisfy even sophisticated needs, people are faced with a conundrum: they must keep spending, and they must be persuaded to spend more. Indeed, much consumer spending today is not aimed at acquiring goods and services but is itself a form of entertainment. A doctor, for instance, is bored with his job and his family and must always have a project to keep himself entertained—a second house that needs renovation, another house at the beach, a farm outside town, an overseas trip for 'professional development', a share in a racehorse, extensions to the family home. This is the pattern of restless overconsumers, who deploy their wealth as a means of avoiding confrontation with the essential meaningless of life that they fear may lie just below the surface. They keep themselves amused by changing the form of their assets.

Consumer society is built on self-delusion. As Juliet Schor observes, 'American consumers are often not conscious of being motivated by social status and are far more likely to attribute such motives to others than themselves. We live with high levels of psychological denial about the connection between our buying habits and the social statements they make'.[29]

It cannot be otherwise, for in creating an identity consumers believe they are living out authentic selves. If they admit that their purchasing decisions are social statements they are admitting that they are living false lives. Most consumer spending is therefore defensive in character; it must be maintained in order to avoid the realisation that we have no place in society, that we do not fit anywhere and so have no real self. Regardless of the longevity of the products purchased, the need to constantly recreate identity is relentless, and this fact is the psychological *sine qua non* for the reproduction of modern consumer capitalism.

Wastefulness is thus essential to sustaining modern consumer capitalism. But it is a new form of waste: it is not the waste of packaging or built-in obsolescence; it is waste arising from the fact that the physical properties of the goods purchased are not the things being consumed. It is the style, the attitude and the image associated with the product that is consumed. The product itself is redundant. The ultimate product would be one with no substance at all but that could nevertheless be displayed; an invisible item whose symbols alone could be attached to the purchaser. Platinum credit cards come close to this. But most display involves the generation of huge amounts of waste, and the natural environment pays the price. There is, therefore, an intimate relationship between the creation of self in consumer capitalism and the destruction of the natural world. This is the unbridgeable gulf between the 'sustainability' that politicians and business people talk about and the deep ecology of the environmentalists. Protecting the natural world requires not only far-reaching changes in the way we use the natural environment: it calls for a radical transformation of our selves.

4

Progress

The idea of progress

The Enlightenment idea of progress is one of the ideological pillars of capitalism. The unspoken assumption motivating modern capitalism is that the world is evolving towards a better, more prosperous future and that the engine of this advancement is economic growth—the expansion of the volume of goods and services at humans' disposal. There may be the occasional interruption to the process, such as periodic recessions, but the momentum is always forwards. Although the idea of progress is little discussed today, the silence serves only to emphasise the idea's universal currency. It pervades our political discourse, the writing of our history, and the consciousness of ordinary people everywhere.

The idea of progress is in fact a new one in human history, perhaps only 200 years old, although its character now reflects the spirit of the golden age that followed the Second World War. Writing in 1851, a French historian confirmed that the new idea had to struggle to replace old conceptions: 'From the beginning of this century the idea of progress has in effect established itself in such a way that in principle it is no longer contested by anyone . . . '[1] A century later, British sociologist Morris Ginsberg noted that, despite its popularity, progress remained difficult to define.[2] In the early 19th century it was given substance by leaps in applied science and technology that were suggestive of infinite inventiveness, but only with Darwin's theories of the later part of the 19th century did the idea of progress acquire an internal logic, the law of evolution. At the same time, enlightened thinkers saw the triumph of science over religious superstition as proof of humankind's ability to create a better future for itself, free from the capriciousness of other-worldly salvation. This conception of meta-history was founded on a belief in the ethical perfectibility of humanity, a belief that provided a powerful philosophical stimulus to movements for social and political reform.

In developing the idea of progress, the intention was to find the impersonal laws that explained the sweep of human history. Hegel has been perhaps the most influential philosopher in this respect. He imagined history as an ineluctable process of expansion of consciousness of freedom or spirit. Eschewing the historians' histories of peoples or of kings, his was a universal history of the evolution of humankind, something that happens over the heads of ordinary mortals. One could either simply watch the world evolve to greater things or, like the social reformers, one could be an active participant, secure in the knowledge that history is on one's side. The more deterministic formulations of Marxism fell into the latter category, as do all theories suggesting that some historical outcome is 'inevitable' or subject to iron laws—including the belief in the inevitability of more economic growth. In a famous passage, Marx wrote, 'Men make their own history, but they do not make it just as they please; [they make it] under circumstances directly found, given and transmitted from the past'.[3] He might have added that they often make it while cleaving to the mistaken ideas of the past, ideas that are contrary to their own interests, so that the 'errors of history' are repeated.

In the first decades of the 20th century belief in progress wavered. Victorian hubris was assailed first by the First World War eruption of savagery, then by the economic collapse of the Depression. A further round of slaughter in the Second World War completed the breakdown. Indeed, between the wars prominent thinkers began to argue that belief in progress would dissolve under the weight of its own contradictions and that the idea should be dismissed as a superstition that is 'nearly worn out'.[4] Blood and misery seemed to call for the idea to be abandoned; after the Battle of the Somme, faith in the perfectibility of humankind became untenable; after Auschwitz, it became a cruel joke. However, by the mid-1950s these doubts were all but forgotten. The awful images of war were supplanted by visions of a new nirvana, one of consumer bliss, captured by the pervasive image of the American housewife. To be sure, a shadow hung over the whole project—the fear that humankind would annihilate itself by thermonuclear war—but the dark side only served to heighten the allure of the light.

High and sustained rates of economic growth through each decade after the war rescued the idea of progress from historical oblivion. But not only was it rescued; it was reconceptualised. Applied science, evolutionary biology and ethics no longer powered the idea. The new engine was more mundane: material advancement would drive progress, and the measure of success became the standard of living. This was convenient, for capitalist firms became the central agency of progress and the entrepreneurs brought their own thinkers to explain their role. Elbowing aside the scientists, philosophers and social reformers, onto this stage walked the new sages of progress, the neoclassical economists.

The neoclassical economists did not have a run free of obstacles. Economists of the Keynesian, Marxist and Institutionalist varieties were sceptical about this new idea of progress, and the neoliberals had to wait until the 1980s and 1990s, and especially for the fall of the Berlin Wall, before claiming complete triumph. Then they could finally dismiss the doubts about the virtues of market capitalism that had been sown, in different ways, by Keynesians and sputniks. As it turned out, the ideological standard bearer of liberal capitalism was not an economist but a little-known political scientist. Francis Fukuyama declared in 1989 that the victory of liberal democracy was so comprehensive that history itself had come to an end. Forms of government other than liberal democracy, and including social democracy, argued Fukuyama, 'were characterized by grave defects and irrationalities that led to their eventual collapse'. However, liberal democracy is 'arguably free from such fundamental internal contradictions'.[5] Although confronted with various practical social problems, he wrote, liberal democracy as an ideal cannot be bested and it is for this reason that history—'understood as a single, coherent, evolutionary process, when taking account of all peoples in all times'—has come to an end.[6]

This argument, and the political emotions it reflected, rested on a belief that history has a purpose, a grand pattern that is revealed with the passage of time and leads to a predefined endpoint. As it happened, Fukuyama adopted the Hegelian view of history as an inexorable process in which consciousness of freedom expands. But the implicit disdain for the lived experience of real people contained the fatal contradiction in his argument, for he concluded, 'This evolutionary process was neither random nor unintelligible, even if it did not proceed in a straight line, and even if it was possible to question whether man was happier or better off as a result of historical "progress"'.[7] In this statement Fukuyama deprived his thesis of meaning: it suggests that there could be other states in which humans are happier but which cannot come about, except temporarily, before being overrun by the juggernaut of history. While the entire philosophical rationale of liberalism, and especially neo-liberalism, is to provide humans with the opportunity to express their free will, Fukuyama's historical process, which has now reached its endpoint, has its own relentless logic, one that deprives people of their freedom to pursue greater happiness.

Real history, freed of deterministic forces (Hegelian, Marxian or other), confirms that free will can be devoted to good or ill, to achieving states superior to liberal democracy or to plunging the world into chaos. In place of free will, Fukuyama substitutes a post-Hegelian driving force for history—science and technology, the motors of economic growth. Hopelessly trapped in the pages of the economics texts, he ends up declaring,

'Technology makes possible the limitless accumulation of wealth, and thus the satisfaction of an *ever-expanding* set of human desires' [emphasis added].[8] Ultimately, Fukuyama's thesis turns out to be no more than a pseudo-philosophical variation on modernisation theory. Science, technology, markets, growth—these forces must take over the world and lead to homogenisation of societies, political systems, consumption patterns and tastes. And on which model does the world converge? That of the United States, of course.

Fukuyama's triumphalism is interesting since his work displayed the contradictions that people experience when they do not consider the goals of actual societies and real people but simply accept the principal assumption of the economics texts and popular political debate—that more money means more happiness. What had triumphed was not democracy but liberalism or, more precisely, neoliberal economics: with the collapse of socialism in Eastern Europe and the convergence of social democracy on Thatcherism in the West, it was the only thing left standing. There seemed no alternative to the pursuit of economic growth through giving full rein to the forces of the market. There had been no challenge to growth, and among Western social democrats there had been no challenge to democracy; it was only the methods of economic organisation that had distinguished the parties.

Oppression and liberation

In the last decades of the 20th century the notion of progress became increasingly associated with ideas of political freedom and liberation. The avatars of the free market have not been afraid to declare that political democracy is the inevitable by-product of economic liberalisation, so that the freeing of markets brings with it the boon of freedom from poverty and tyranny. Whatever the historical merits of the argument—and there are few— freedom from political oppression and material deprivation has presented neoliberalism with a dilemma: will citizens be happy exercising their freedoms simply through occasional trips to the polling station and frequent visits to the shopping mall, or will the democratic impulse take them into uncharted territory where perhaps the values that underpin neoliberalism will themselves come under challenge? It is hard to avoid the conclusion that the forces unleashed by affluence and democracy are getting out of hand, at least from the viewpoint of consumer capitalism. German sociologist Ulrich Beck is one of the most acute observers of the historical process: '. . . changing values and acceptance of democracy go hand in hand. An inner kinship exists between the values of self-determination and the ideal of democracy'.[9]

Taking democracy seriously means accepting the right to personal self-determination. Yet the dominant conservative view is comfortable with only one form of self-determination— personal choice in the marketplace—which, I argue, is a counterfeit form of self-determination. Beck has launched an attack on 'conservative wailers' of the moralising right for their attempts to constrain the historical evolution of democracy, attempts that are all the more surprising for conservatives who promote the free market as the last stage of freedom. Conservative resistance to the demand for self-determination conflates the pursuit of self-determination (individualisation) with the pursuit of selfish interests (individualism). The tragedy of market economics is that if it did in fact accurately reflect the essential motivation of human life—an anthropic version of Nature 'red in tooth and claw'—we would soon find ourselves living a nightmare. The makers of post-apocalyptic films such as *Mad Max* and *Waterworld* recognised that it is only selflessness, love for others, that stands between us and the hell of rational economic man.

If we consider the evolution of the democratic impulse through its historical stages, the moral decline bemoaned by the conservatives is no more than a period of transition, in which the traditional expectations and roles that defined industrial capitalism are disintegrating and something new is emerging. The rejection of traditional standards, expectations and stereotypes represented by the various trends and movements dating from the 1960s—the sexual revolution, the counter-culture, and the women's movement—was a manifestation of the longing for self-determination. Democracy, combined with the arrival of widespread material abundance in the West, has for the first time provided the opportunity for the mass of ordinary people to pursue self-actualisation. The political demand for democracy of earlier generations has become a personal demand for freedom to find one's own path, to 'write one's own biography'. The constraints of socially imposed roles have weakened, oppression based on gender and race is no longer tenable, and the daily struggle for survival has for most people disappeared. All across the industrialised world bewildered people have been asking, 'What do we do now?'[10] Or, as the ethicist Peter Singer has put it, 'How should I live?'. For if the life-determining constraints of

105

class, gender and race have by and large fallen away, and the threat of poverty has for most been dissolved by decades of economic growth, the ordinary individual has, for the first time in history, a true choice.

The democratic impulse—which to date has taken the form of collective struggles to be free of autocrats, plutocrats and oligarchs—has segued into something else, a search for authentic identity, for self-actualisation, for the achievement of true individuality. Some have gone straight to the known sources in various spiritual traditions. But most have ended up seeking a proxy identity in the form of commodity consumption, consumer capitalism's answer to meaninglessness. Others have looked for the answer in drugs. People continue to pursue more wealth and consume at ever higher levels because they do not know how better to answer the question 'What do I do now?'. The agents of the marketing society have seized on the primal search for authentic identity to sell more gym shoes, cars, mobile phones and home furnishings. And what happens at the level of the individual translates into society's preoccupation with growth, an autistic behavioural pattern reinforced daily by the platitudes of the commentators and the politicians. But this state of affairs can be sustained for only so long. Despite its extraordinary success over the last four or five decades, the marketing project must ultimately fail: in the last instance, a pair of designer jeans cannot satisfy the deeper urge to make sense of a life.

Drawing the decisive distinction between individualisation (self-determination) and individualism (selfishness), Beck succinctly poses the great question of our age: 'How can the longing for self-determination be brought into harmony with the equally important longing for shared community? How can one simultaneously be individualistic and merge with the group?'.[11] Finding the answer to the question is all the more difficult in an era of consumer capitalism, where the enormous resources of marketing are devoted to convincing us that the answer lies in the consumption process. Yet the true answer has long been known by the sages: the two are reconciled once we understand that genuine self-determination can be had only by committing oneself to others. As Beck reminds us, commitment to others does not necessarily mean total sacrifice of self. For most people, the art of living lies in balancing the two. Besides, if active compassion can be self-realisation, then looking to the interests of others is 'self-interested'.

In the marketing society, power and oppression are no longer concerned predominantly with the domination of one group by another but are bound up with what people do to themselves. For most citizens, the fruits of growth have provided the means to seize emancipation, yet few have availed themselves of the opportunity. As is suggested later, this irony is perhaps most stark in the success of the women's movement, where progress towards liberation was diverted into equality in work and consumption. While power, oppression and resistance were in an earlier era played out in the arena of production, now they are played out in the arena of consumption and the wider polity. This should not be taken to mean that the exercise of power has become wholly depersonalised by absorption into 'the system'. As Andre Gorz argues, '... the dominated class is everywhere ... it is no longer definable by its position in the process of production ...

domination is exerted over people outside enterprises as well as inside them, both in their work and in their lives outside work'.[12]

Industrial struggles still occur, but they are rarely life-or-death struggles. To be sure, certain groups in society are disparaged and victimised—the homeless, the long-term unemployed, people with disabilities, indigenous people—but the system has no structural interest in this sort of oppression, except perhaps a fiscal one.

For most workers, the modern economy and labour market provide some degree of autonomy that makes them much less subject to the dictates of the boss than they were in the past. This is more the case for some types of workers than for others, and it holds even in the face of attempts to remove protections in labour laws. In the West wage slavery belongs to another era. But if oppression is the opposite of liberation, and liberation means a life in which each person can live out their full potential and achieve true autonomy, we remain oppressed. Such a view is, of course, alien to the enlightened advocate of neoliberalism—after all, haven't modern social movements swept away all the oppressions of the past? The sexual revolution freed us from our Victorian inhibitions; the women's movement freed women from role stereotyping; gay liberation allowed free expression of sexual preference; and the civil rights movement eliminated institutionalised racism. Conservatives fulminated and progressive people celebrated.

The social movements of the post-war period have, however, for the most part represented no threat to consumer capitalism. Indeed, the counter-culture, the civil rights movement, the women's movement, and even the mainstream parts of the environment movement have served to reinvigorate it. Post-war rebellions against oppression have worked in the interests of consumer capitalism because they have swept away ancient cultural and religious barriers to the most insidious form of oppression. This is the oppression implicit in sublimation of the self in pursuit of wealth, fame and social success, a form of oppression that is readily embraced. In the end, liberation is denied those who invest their lives in external reward.

This is not just a matter of personal choice: capitalism conspires to ensure that external rewards will triumph over the urge to liberation. In a famous passage on the conquering power of capitalism, Marx declared:

> All fixed, fast-frozen relations, with their train of ancient and venerable prejudices and opinions, are swept away, all new-formed ones become antiquated before they can ossify. All that is solid melts into air, all that is holy is profaned, and man is at last compelled to face with sober senses, his real conditions of life, and his relations with his kind.[13]

Marx's declaration was in some respects premature, since pre-industrial social conventions and conservative attitudes continued to impose constraints on the full manifestation of market capitalism for a century after publication of *The Communist Manifesto*. It is now becoming clear that the Sixties generation tilled the ground for the neoliberal reforms and 'turbo-capitalism' of the 1980s and 1990s. Railing against the conventions of their parents, the counter-culture tore down the social structures of conservatism that, for all their stultifying oppressiveness, held the market in check. The demands for freedom in private life, for freedom from the fetters of career and family, and for freedom of sexual expression were noble in themselves, but it is now evident that demolition of the customary social structures did not create a society of free individuals. Instead, it created an opportunity for the marketers to substitute material consumption and manufactured lifestyles for the ties of social tradition. In the face of revolutionary changes in social attitudes in the West, consumer capitalism has remained unruffled. Indeed, each new social revolution has provided an opportunity for consumer capitalism to rejuvenate itself. Both the counter-culture and environmentalism contained within them seeds of revolt, but they were effortlessly co-opted, so that now those who are inclined can simply buy an alternative lifestyle.

The women's movement attacked the social and family conventions that kept women in the kitchen. The family built around the male breadwinner undoubtedly denied women the opportunity to spread their wings, but it also conditioned the labour market to operate on the assumption that workers had family responsibilities. Men formed trade unions to fight for limits on working hours, security of employment, and carefully regulated pay structures. When workers demanded a 'living wage' that could sustain a married man and his wife and children, the moral argument had wide appeal. This world of security in which people knew their roles as well as their social responsibilities has gone. The counter-culture took the hatchet to it long before the ideologues of the free market decided that we could all be richer if the labour market were deregulated. The counter-culture had its wish. Gone are the stuffy constraints of career expectations, nine-to-five regimentation and the life mapped out by the corporation's hierarchy. Now workers are free-floating commodities in the labour market, often employed casually or on contract, the only consideration being their measurable contribution to the firm's productivity. The future of each worker in the firm counts for little, although, as is argued in Chapter 6, this system also contains the seeds of its own demise.

So Margaret Thatcher should be thankful to Alan Ginsberg and Timothy Leary. The counter-culture tuned in, turned on and dropped out, but only long enough to sweep aside the social conventions that had provided the moral constraint on the amoral urgings of consumer capitalism. Born of the middle classes, the standard-bearers of the counter-culture returned with a vengeance in the shape of 'bourgeois bohemians', or bobos—switched-on share traders, professionals, journalists and executives in e-businesses.[14] Bobos see no inconsistency between trading shares and sporting a ponytail. They feel they are making a personal statement by drinking coffee at a cafe decked out in 'Third World chic', unconscious of the fact that the manufactured style is alien to both rich and poor in the Third World. They support the oppressed of the Third World, but only so long as their support does not impinge on their own lifestyles. The best and most savvy marketers understand the psychology of the counter-culture; they are, after all, products of it. For the counter-culture was never a revolt against capitalism: it was a revolt against the social conservatism that held capitalism back.

These social changes can be tracked through the demographics of the labour market. The transformation since the 1960s has been seismic in its social implications; in terms of their speed and social impact, the changes have rarely been matched in human history. The entry of large numbers of women into the labour market and the greater educational opportunities for girls (to the point where they now out-perform boys)—perhaps the greatest achievements of feminism—are inseparable from the changing patterns of fertility and nuptial arrangements. In Western Europe in the seventies, nine out of ten 30-year-old women had married; today, the figure is around one in two. Four in ten women today wait until after their 30th birthday to have a baby; in the seventies it was one in ten.[15]

Women are postponing starting families until they have established themselves in the labour market. This does not represent an aversion to having children; it is a result of joining the workforce in their twenties. When young women leave school they envisage marriage and motherhood for themselves, but in their twenties they are exposed to the market. As a result they become more cautious and recognise the financial and career risks associated with motherhood. And so they delay motherhood and have fewer children. In most countries of Europe and in Japan the fertility rate has fallen sharply since the 1970s—to well below the replacement rate. Women today know they do not have to rely on a good marriage to build a life of material comfort. Gaining a university degree can be a safer option. If your husband leaves, you might be left without companionship and with extra responsibilities for the children, but you will have retained an income-earning capacity, professional respect, and a sense of self that does not dissolve with the marriage. Independence has its benefits as well as its costs.

It is fitting that Germaine Greer should now shatter the feminist dream in her book *The Whole Woman*. For all the advances in education and employment and for all the dramatic changes in attitudes, women have now become paid-up members of the market system. They have achieved equality so that they can feel alienated and exploited in the way men do. They sought liberation but settled for equality. Greer might have gone further and said that women wanted liberation but were bought off with equality. Women can never be liberated until men are too, and neither can be free when they are active and willing participants in consumer culture. In the 1950s middle-class respectability may have been oppressive but it carried with it a certain deference. Women are the subject of far more sexual objectification now than they were in the 1950s, although men have become more adept at concealing it. And even the need to conceal has been discarded by the crass exploitation of 'girl power'. Why should a young man pretend that he doesn't lust after the young woman who has just burned him off at the traffic lights, when nubile popstars thrust their groins at the camera and declare 'more power to us'?

As happened with the counter-culture of the 1960s, feminism has been co-opted. Greer observes, 'What none of us noticed was that the ideal of liberation was fading out with the word'. The liberation of women from oppression was understood by the early feminists as freedom from internalisation of self-hatred and self-denigration. Algerian anti-colonialist author Franz Fanon and South African black consciousness activist Steve Biko understood that oppression runs deep: while discriminatory laws can be changed, the internalisation of oppression is far more insidious. Colonialism was threatened by liberation struggles, patriarchy by feminism, and segregation by the civil rights movement. But what sort of people would be left by liberation? The results of feminist struggles have become painfully clear: 'Women's liberation did not see the female's potential in terms of the male's actual; the visionary feminists of the late sixties and early seventies knew that women could never find freedom by agreeing to live the lives of unfree men'.[16]

Patriarchy became interpreted as a sort of add-on to consumer capitalism that could be dealt with while leaving the system intact. Women's liberation turned out to be a superb marketing opportunity. Here was a huge new demographic that wanted something different—commodities that would express how the new woman felt about herself.

Patriarchy reflects a particular approach to power and its exercise, to social structure, to systems of reward and punishment, to ways of knowing the world and the self. If any large group were to step outside the marketing society they would indeed pose a severe threat to that society. A handful of hippies and radical feminists can be accommodated, but for half the population to demand real liberation and the opportunity to seek authentic individuality would be intolerable. It is not so much that 'the economy' is the centre around which all else, including gender relations, revolves; the centre is the social structuring of the means by which people can strive to realise their potential.

In arguing that the women's movement sought liberation but settled for equality, Greer is asking once more about the nature of oppression. Patriarchy was not just something that men did to women; rather, it was a system of self-understanding embedded in a structure: 'Equality is cruel to women because it requires them to duplicate behaviours that they find profoundly alien and disturbing. Men like the masculine world they have built for themselves . . . In constructing its male elite, masculinist society contrives to be cruel to most men, all women and all children'.[17]

Gender equality has meant, above all, unfettered opportunity for women to create themselves in the images invented for them by the marketers. Whether a woman is a dutiful housewife or a kick-arse careerist is a matter of indifference to the marketers, as long as she continues to spend. There is no difference between an advertising campaign that appeals to the image of the nurturing, caring mother and one that targets the power-dressed professional; indeed, the cleverer campaigns manage to combine both. Each is just a demographic; the only difference is that the independent professional believes she is more in control of her life when she is deciding what to buy. Greer has a cruel term for it—'lifestyle feminism':

> . . . the kind of feminism that sees getting membership of the MCC or the Garrick Club as a triumph is lifestyle feminism that gives tacit support to a system that oppresses women worldwide. A 'new feminism' that celebrates the right (i.e. duty) to be pretty in an array of floaty dresses and little suits put together for starvation wages by adolescent girls in Asian sweat-shops is no feminism at all.[18]

Greer is right to say that feminism is incompatible with consumerism, because feminism, as a form of liberation, is about being true to one's real self, while consumerism creates and sustains a false sense of the self, of the world and of one's relationship to it. Equality is good for the market. It has meant a growing and better qualified workforce; it has destroyed old-fashioned ideas that employers need to pay enough to support a family; it has helped turn nurturing households into nodes of consumption; it has hastened the development of lifestyle thinking; and it has exposed a much larger proportion of the population to the direct influence of the advertisers. Mrs Thatcher has much to thank feminism for.

Globalisation

At the broadest level, globalisation is seen as either the most powerful contemporary source of progress or a new and insidious form of oppression. It is usually characterised as a process in which mighty economic forces increasingly link all corners of the world in a network dominated by, and operated in the interests of, large corporations. The process, which began in the 1970s, has seen potent economic actors, in tandem with political and cultural ones, impose their will on others who are seen to be passive victims. It is the product of the transformation of international institutions and domestic economic policies, which has facilitated almost unrestricted mobility of commodities and capital. Trade has been liberalised, international capital flows have been freed up and currencies have been floated, and all of these have been justified on the grounds that they will improve the rate of economic growth.

Perhaps the most dramatic feature of the modern globalised world is the extraordinary size and influence of international capital markets. Their power is usually measured in economic terms—their ability to change the status of a whole economy

within days, or even hours. Definitions of globalisation tend to
be specifically economic ('the increasing organisation of finance,
investment, production, distribution and marketing in a way that
pertains to or embraces the world'[19]) or broadly social ('the
widening, deepening and speeding up of worldwide interconnec-
tedness in all aspects of contemporary social life'[20]), perhaps
focusing on cause and effect in turn. These are the terms in which
globalisation has been viewed both in popular debate and in academic discourse. But such a simple explanation is implausible,
not least because it leaves unasked the most important question.
Why, at least until very recently, has globalisation met with so
little resistance?

Notwithstanding the role of technological factors, which
follow a largely autonomous path, the dimensions of globalisation could have been very different. Globalisation has gone as far
as it has only because political decision makers, in countries with
both democratic and authoritarian governments, have made a
series of decisions to remove obstacles from its path—including
decisions affecting trade, investment, capital markets, fiscal and
monetary policies, public ownership and the operation of international institutions, all designed to reflect the wishes of the
market. Apart from decisions to dismantle existing barriers, there
have been important decisions, explicit or implicit, to resist pressure to put obstacles in the way of globalisation. The attempts in
Malaysia and Mexico in more recent years to restrict capital flows
raise the question of why more extensive attempts were not made
earlier. If globalisation has such widespread negative effects, why
have people, especially in Western nations, not done more to
stop it?

The ideological power of the forces of globalisation is little discussed, yet it provides the beginning of the answer to the question of why globalisation has met with so little resistance. 'The markets' are not politically neutral. They constantly make judgments, or at least their actors make judgments, about the political desirability of all manner of policy decisions by national governments. For instance, they have a strong preference for measures that reduce inflation at the expense of higher unemployment, for measures that reduce public spending in ways that diminish welfare provision, and for precedence to be given to 'development' over environmental protection. While on the face of it the objective is to maximise returns on investments, in fact the pursuit of profit is not based on 'objective' information: it is based on political and ideological choices. To illustrate, the markets and their apologists in the economics profession consistently ignore evidence that contradicts their preference for small government, fiscal restraint and low inflation. Globalisation is thus not just the spread of corporate and financial activity: it is the spread of political ideas backed by economic power.

Although this is suggestive of the reasons why elites have acquiesced in the face of globalising forces, it does not explain why ordinary people have been complicit, albeit in many instances with reservations. The barrage of pro-market propaganda in the media, popular confusion about what is happening, and a pervasive sense of powerlessness all undoubtedly contribute. At another level, however, globalisation represents not just the export and imposition of economic policies built on neoliberal orthodoxy. It represents the export of a culture and a psychological disposition, one based on growth fetishism, compulsive consumption, and thoughtless exploitation of the natural world. In rich countries, popular scepticism was overruled by the repeated claim that deregulation in all its forms would increase growth, incomes and consumer choice. In the Third World, while many nations achieved political independence after the Second World War, their leaders had absorbed the most intoxicating idea of their colonisers, the belief that the first objective of any state should be economic growth. Colonialism could not have left a more powerful legacy, one that has morphed from the developmentalism of the 1960s into full-blown consumer capitalism. If the income has not trickled down, the ideology certainly has.

At its heart, therefore, globalisation is not so much about the deepening of global economic and financial networks or the extension of the international reach of corporations; it is about the restless spread of the ideology of growth and consumer capitalism. The instrumental processes of globalisation—the opening up of trade, the emergent power of financial markets, the transnationalisation of corporations, and international economic coordination—are the mechanisms by which a historically and culturally specific ideology, constituted as an independent force, has spread and colonised the world, including the 'communist' world. While the motive force is the accumulation of wealth through profit seeking, the ideology draws its legitimacy from the core belief that human wellbeing is advanced above all else by increasing the quantity and quality of goods and services consumed by individuals. This gives privileged place to all activities and policies that promise an increase in the rate of economic growth. Parallel with this formal set of beliefs are cultural forms of behaviour that place enormous emphasis on consumption as the foundation of lifestyle. This is why there has been so little resistance to globalisation: people from Beijing to Berlin, Boston to Beirut, have been persuaded by the ideology of consumer capitalism, that economic growth is the path to happiness and that unfettered markets will maximise that growth. In other words, globalisation has succeeded because people are besotted by consumption.

Belief in the power of growth and consumption is in turn buttressed by an instrumentalist attitude to the natural world, an attitude in which the environment is characterised as providing 'resources' that have value only because, and to the extent that, they contribute to human welfare as measured through market activity. This ideology conceives of the natural world as a more or less infinite source of material inputs into the production process and a more or less infinite sink for absorbing wastes, so that exploitation of it is not only a right but almost a duty. This reflects an approach to Nature whose genesis lies deep in the cultural roots of Western society, stretching back at least as far as the foundation of Christianity.[21]

Like growth itself, globalisation is now implanted in people's minds as a force beyond human control. It is remarkable how widely it is believed that economic expansion is inevitable. This view is accepted uncritically by even the most progressive people, people who are quite willing to concede that more growth will not make us any better off. 'The Economy' has assumed such supremacy in people's minds that it has taken on the character of a law of nature, like evolution. It is as if The Economy has broken away from human society and assumed a life of its own. We attempt to exert some control over it through macro-economic policy, but in the end it is beyond us. This objectification of the economy is a relatively recent development, although it has an older political precursor, the belief that 'we can't stop progress'. Before the 1970s fewer people believed that growth was inevitable; it was popularly believed that sustained productivity growth would soon take us to a time of plenty, when we would all be satiated and the need to work would sharply decline.

Several arguments are used in support of the belief that growth is inevitable. They are the arguments that will be used to suggest that the 'post-growth society' advocated in this book is utopian. The economics texts share at least one thing with popular wisdom—that human desire is insatiable and people will always want to increase their incomes. This is obviously a culturally specific belief that has been presented as 'human nature'. Anyone with a knowledge of pre-industrial societies knows that, while greed has a very long history, the idea that human desire for material goods is inherently limitless is contradicted by the anthropological facts, including (as discussed in Chapter 8) some anthropological facts of the 21st century. But perhaps a more compelling explanation for the fact that so many people believe that economic growth is inevitable is simply that the mantra is so often intoned, and all authoritative people seem to believe it. So rarely is the inevitability of growth questioned that most people immediately become defensive when asked to follow the position through. Maybe the belief in the inevitability of growth is the counterpart of the consumerist dream: it is convenient to believe that growth will never end because such a belief opens up the possibility of unrestrained expansion in our lifetimes, thus validating our guilty acquisitiveness.

5

Politics

The Third Way

In the last decade social democratic and labour parties have been dominated by the ideas of the Third Way. The term was coined as part of the reinvention of social democracy in response to the wave of neoliberalism that captured the world in the 1980s and early 1990s. Uneasy with the harshness of Thatcherism and with the untenability of socialism, advocates of the Third Way looked for a means of grafting traditional social democratic concern for equality and social justice onto an economic system based on free markets. Neoliberal economics seemed to have destroyed the case for greater social ownership and collective provision of many services. Although social democratic and labour parties had long since rejected the corrupt forms of socialism that had been imposed on Eastern Europe, it was the fall of the Berlin Wall in

1989 that seemed finally to bring down the curtain on an era in which even mild forms of collectivism could be pursued as an alternative to capitalism rampant. Within those parties, the left wing fell silent for want of ideas and was vanquished, while the 'pragmatists' of the Right argued that the parties must flow with the neoliberal tide and try to channel it so that traditional principles were protected. Thus emerged the Third Way, a political program described eloquently by Anthony Giddens in his 1998 book *The Third Way: the renewal of social democracy*.

As a political program, the Third Way implicitly accepts the two most important ideas of the First Way—that the principal objective of government should be to increase the rate of economic growth and that the best way to achieve this objective is through the free operation of private markets. Certainly, it is conceded by Giddens and others, in some situations constraints must be placed on markets, but this does not imply criticism of the free market as such. Having accepted these fundamentals of the First Way, the Third Way has had difficulty finding a rationale that differentiates it in any substantive way from neoliberalism.

One of the clearest statements of the Third Way can be found in a collection of essays by the Demos Foundation, a London think tank closely aligned with Prime Minister Tony Blair. The editors of the 1998 volume, *Tomorrow's Politics: the Third Way and beyond*, noted that the Centre Left—which they defined so broadly as to include the then Clinton administration in Washington—had taken government throughout much of the Western world, but that to do so the Third Way 'has had to accept some of the Right's agenda'. Consequently:

the political contest is focused on how to balance prosperity with social inclusion, capitalism with community, how to modernise welfare systems, public services and labour markets, how to deepen democracy and how to connect progressive politics with the imperative of ecological sustainability.[1]

The implications are that prosperity (which means sustaining economic growth) is at odds with social inclusion, but only in the absence of ameliorative measures; that capitalism erodes community, but can be made consistent with it; and that welfare systems, public services and labour markets need to be modernised, where 'modernisation' means changed so that they do not stand in the way of the globalised world. The shallowness of democracy is not explained and is definitely not attributed to the convergence of parties of the Left on the conservatives' program.

As this suggests, the central ideas of the Third Way remain slippery, although some have attempted to define it as a philosophy with three cornerstones:

the idea that government should promote equal opportunity for all while granting special privilege to none; an ethic of mutual responsibility that equally rejects the politics of entitlement and the politics of social abandonment; and, a new approach to governing that empowers citizens to act for themselves.[2]

While this triplet seems to match the pronouncements of Britain's Labour government and social democratic governments in Germany, it is also entirely consistent with the views of modern conservative parties. It is not inconsistent to accept the prevailing system and at the same time put forward policies to mitigate some of its negative social and environmental effects, as long as one believes that the undesirable effects are not caused by anything fundamental to the system. As soon as one begins to reflect on the philosophy of the Third Way it becomes apparent that it is not based on any critical analysis of modern capitalism; thus a critique of the Third Way as a political philosophy must begin from what the philosophy fails to say rather than what it says it stands for. In contrast with traditional social democratic and socialist programs, one looks in vain for any discussion of classes, exploitation, the influence of the profit motive, the power of transnational corporations, the division of labour, the myth of free markets, the alienation of consumer society, or even the roots of unsustainable development and the forms of patriarchy.

The absence of any challenge to consumer capitalism means that much of the Third Way's political agenda has now been adopted quite comfortably by conservative parties that are moving back from a hard-line position as the damage inflicted by the decade of neoliberal policies becomes a political liability. The absence of a rationale led Giddens himself to make the astonishing admission that governments throughout Europe claiming to represent the Left were making policy on the run and that practical policies are not guided by any political principles: 'In the UK, as in many countries at the moment, theory lags behind practice . . . governments claiming to represent the left are creating policy on the hoof. Theoretical flesh needs to be put on the skeleton of their policy-making . . . '[3] In other words, we know what we want to do but we lack a justification for doing it.

Although Giddens was writing in the late 1990s, no progress has been made towards putting theoretical flesh on the policy skeleton—except perhaps in the area of 'social capital' (the accretion of networks, norms and trust that binds communities together), itself a contested idea claimed as much by conservatives as by social democrats.

The aversion to social criticism means that advocates of the Third Way shy away from discussion of the motive force of political and social change—that is, the sources, forms and distribution of power in modern society. Traditionally, socialists understood power as deriving from ownership of capital, and oppression, injustice and inequality as arising from the struggle between capital and labour. Although most would agree that this is a simplification that conceals as much as it reveals, it nevertheless focuses on something fundamental to the structure of society. But in the Third Way no fundamentals are challenged; the world of the Third Way is characterised by complexity rather than conflict, and it is difficult to avoid the conclusion that talking about complexity serves as a means of avoiding consideration of conflict.

Giddens is quite explicit about the Third Way's desire to reject class and avoid any discussion of power relations that may be built into the social structure. He writes that 'Third Way politics is one-nation politics',[4] so that we are all united in one nation. We may have our disagreements but nothing fundamental divides us. The implication is that social and environmental problems are not the result of exploitation but of ignorance; when enough people understand, our problems will be resolved. The response to ignorance is education and persuasion, not compulsion. This suggests that when business organisations resist proposed new laws to cut greenhouse gas emissions or increase social security payments it is because they do not yet understand that the new laws are in the interests of us all. The Third Way is determined to be pragmatic, to avoid sterile ideologies, and to embrace change rather than resist it. It does not have a 'world view', only some practical policies to make the world a better place. It is apparent that the conscious rejection of ideology serves a political function. But by eschewing a world view the Third Way does not make itself innocent: contrary to the positivists of the economics profession, there is no economic system that somehow stands outside ideology. If the Third Way does not have its own world view, it has nothing to separate itself from the prevailing world view and must therefore share it. This is why many on the Left see the Third Way as in fact little more than an apologia for the prevailing system and its advocates as supporters of a system that is responsible for creating the very things they condemn—inequality, injustice and environmental decline.

In politics today it is *de rigueur* to claim that everyone will be a winner, and Third Way politicians have proved masters of conflict avoidance. Yet far-reaching social changes involve often-titanic political struggles in which progress requires the defeat of entrenched forces. It is naive to expect otherwise. It remains true that, although power structures are complex and multifaceted, the locus of power in modern society lies in the business community and especially those segments that created and prospered from the neoliberal policies of Margaret Thatcher, Ronald Reagan and their followers. Unless we are to resort to the fatuous escape route of 'expanding the pie so that everyone can have more', we must confront the realities of economic and political power. Indeed, we have had enough years of witnessing Third Way politicians warming the seats of power to know that serious attempts at social reform have run into trenchant opposition and that the representatives of the Third Way have repeatedly sacrificed the boldness of social change for the moderation of practical politics. Of course, the Third Way champions' unwillingness to consider power is a predisposition they share with the defenders of neoliberalism. Nor has the Third Way challenged the model of human wellbeing on which the economics texts are based. It has not questioned the utilitarian philosophy of modern economics and the marketing society; it implicitly accepts the philosophy built around *homo economicus*, rational economic man, and all the anthropocentrism, individualism, materialism, and celebration of competition implied by it.

Democracy itself is subtly undermined by the refusal to consider the nature of power and the glib assumption that ultimate power lies in unfettered consumption behaviour. Democracy asserts itself when great issues that demand collective decisions grip a nation. In practice, governments represent the people best when they are protecting the people's rights against threats from the powerful and providing for things that are best provided collectively—defence, roads, schooling, health care and environmental protection. The act of collective provision is something that citizens do for one another. In contrast with the comatose sovereign consumer of neoliberalism, *democracy needs something to do*. By ceding so much decision making to the private choices of consumers in markets, electors have been transformed into political automatons. The capitulation of social democratic parties to the neoliberal idea has been central to this, so that the Third Way serves as a sort of civic tranquilliser, the post-modern opium of the people.

Advocates of the Third Way argue that the pursuit of ideology is old-fashioned, that society today is not marked by class division but by a 'messy plurality', and that politics is no longer the art of struggles for class dominance and social transformation.[5] The politics of struggle has been superseded, writes Giddens, by the politics of lifestyle, and the real concerns of 'life politics' involve questions of autonomy and self-expression.[6] There is some truth in this perception of modern attitudes and politics insofar as the dynamic of modern capitalism has shifted from the production to the consumption sphere. The problem is the uncritical acceptance of 'life politics' by advocates of the Third Way. There is no analysis of why people have retreated to lifestyle and no discussion of whether the messy plurality is a surface manifestation of deeper, systemic social changes. The Third Way seems to be saying that if people want lifestyle that is what we must give them, without asking what forces lie behind the pursuit of identity and self-worth through lifestyle choices and brand association and how these perceptions are created and manipulated in the marketing society. Thus the 'life politics' of the Third Way is precisely the politics that suits the consumer society: it focuses on manufactured identity and the flim-flam of marketing, rather than the deeper urges of humanity. It is the politics of the masses caught in a web spun by corporations and their publicists. Nowhere in the writings on the Third Way can one find an analysis of how social structures condition thinking; nor can one find discussion of class consciousness or false consciousness or any inkling of why people believe what they do. The political superficiality of the Third Way is the ideal counterpart of the emptiness of modern consumer capitalism.

Underlying all this is a belief that people are free to choose what is best for them, in exactly the same way that the economics texts cleave to consumer sovereignty as the guarantee that in free markets people will get what they want. But what the idea of consumer sovereignty and the political individualism of the Third Way refuse to recognise is that people's preferences are not created *ex nihilo*: they are formed by the society they live in—which in the present case means in large measure and increasingly by the messages of the marketing society. Because the advocates of the Third Way have no social critique, they imagine that people are free to pursue their life goals and to 'create themselves', ostensibly from nothing. In the post-modern world people create their own selves, but they do not create them just as they please: they create them under circumstances and with materials made and transmitted by the ideology of growth fetishism and the marketing machine.

The Third Way is adamant that, rather than deciding for people what they want, its purpose is to provide everyone with the opportunity to express and satisfy their personal desires. A deeper critique would acknowledge that, because our desires are so bounded by the ideology of growth fetishism and so concealed by layers of images and distorted associations created by decades of marketing, until we individually and collectively stop to examine ourselves we do not know what is in our interests.[7] In the Third Way, the model citizen is the highly educated, flexible, mobile worker—'symbolic analysts' or 'bourgeois bohemians',[8] best represented perhaps by Tony Blair himself. We might call this model 'Third Way Man', a caricature that reaches its zenith with the invention of the 'wired worker', the exemplary worker of the information age who transcends the class struggle and stands as the model citizen, the Stakhanovite of history's end.[9] While one could venture a sociological critique of this type and argue that it will always represent only a small proportion of the population, the real question that must be asked is whether high incomes, professional mobility, disdain for community, and inflated self-image actually make Third Way Man happy. For if they are not happy, why would government policy attempt to create the conditions for them to multiply?

Faced with the increasingly untenable nature of socialism and state ownership in the post-war period, and the absence of any coherent alternative to the crushing force of the neoliberal policy establishment, many social democrats felt they could do little more than fight a rearguard action as one after another of the pillars of the post-war social democratic consensus was knocked down. The tragedy was that so many of the most influential social democrats just surrendered. Instead of searching for a creative response to the new dispensation, they embraced Mrs Thatcher—secretly, of course. As the conservative commentator Geoffrey Wheatcroft observed in 1999, 'Intelligent British Tories have quietly recognised that Blair's New Labour is Thatcher's greatest triumph',[10] an assessment confirmed in 2002 by Peter Mandelson, often seen as Tony Blair's svengali, when he declared, 'We are all Thatcherites now'.[11]

The creeping capitulation of social democratic parties led to an extraordinary bipartisanship on economic policy—that is, on the questions that mattered most. As opposition to privatisation, free trade, competition policy and deregulation of the financial sector fell away, an elaborate dance of deception began. The gap between the conservative and social democratic parties became one of product differentiation rather than ideology and, just as product differentiation and brand loyalty are marketing concepts, so political parties began to hire marketing specialists to help them sell their messages. In the same way that clever marketing is required to persuade sceptical consumers that one brand of soap powder is radically different from other virtually identical brands, so political parties now hire experts to persuade sceptical voters that one party is radically different from its opponent. Increasingly, modern social democratic politics is the politics of politicians who are not sure what they stand for but who employ advertising agencies to convince us that they stand for something. Today both conservative and social democratic parties complain that the other party has stolen its policies. So little that is fundamental separates them that almost any policy could be found in the platform of either party. The adoption of a particular policy is determined not by consistency with some broad ideology but by whoever thought of it first. With the advent of the Third Way, politics made a transition from ideas to personalities. The spin doctor replaced the policy analyst; the party platform can be found buried beneath the media strategy; image management substituted for bold reform; and choosing words became more important than choosing actions. 'Staying on message' means avoiding debate.

The disappearance of substantive difference between the conservative and social democratic parties has meant that both parties are more likely to attract careerists and opportunists instead of people committed to principles. We now see rising to prominence younger politicians who in their twenties were courted by both sides. They could have comfortably jumped either way but made a decision on the basis of which party would better facilitate personal advancement. The triumph of neo-liberalism and the new right has led social commentators to conclude that people have lost interest in politics and that this is a threat to democracy. Writes Giddens, 'Political ideas today seem to have lost their capacity to inspire and political leaders their ability to lead'.[12] The loss of political idealism that Giddens bemoans is itself the product of the convergence of Third Way politics on neoliberalism. Third Way politicians say they want to revive political engagement by creating a realisable vision for a better future. But the Third Way has inspired no mass following because it does not know what it stands for—at least not beyond the things it does not want to talk about and the faith in free markets and materialism that it shares with its opponents. The result is that people are staying away from the polling booths, voting on the basis of personalities rather than policies, or seeking out alternatives to the traditional parties.

The power of economic ideas

The unwillingness of the champions of the Third Way to consider power is a disposition they share with the defenders of neo-liberalism. Nor has the Third Way challenged the model of human wellbeing on which the economics texts are based. It has not questioned the utilitarian philosophy of modern economics and the marketing society, the sovereignty of the consumer and all the anthropocentrism, individualism, materialism and celebration of competition implied by it. It has not confronted the simple belief in progress, and it has everywhere succumbed to the allure of technology and economic internationalism. Neoliberalism could not persuade everyone that markets are inherently good and government intervention bad, but one of its legacies has been to persuade almost everyone that once markets are opened up governments become powerless to change things. In other words, while one might not like neoliberal policies, once they are implemented they are irreversible. A parallel belief is that globalisation has created international economic forces that have emasculated governments, and the consequent diminution of the power of the state has destroyed for ever the appeal of 'old-style social democracy'. The traditional values of social democracy may remain admirable, but in the new globalised world those who still adhere to its political program are hopelessly utopian.

According to this view, modern politics is no more than a reconciliation with global economic reality. Giddens, for example, writes that the Third Way 'refers to a framework of thinking and policy making that seeks to adapt social democracy to a world that has changed fundamentally over the past two or three decades'.[13] Above all, it is the strictures on government that make the Third Way necessary, for globalisation has robbed social democracy of its most effective weapon, the power of the state. Of course, it is a great comfort to neoliberals that, whatever one might think about the desirability of globalisation, there seems to be nothing that can be done about it. If any government attempted to resist the trend it would be severely punished by 'the markets' and compelled to fall into line. Staying in line requires governments to pursue a suite of economic policies that keep the markets happy—fiscal discipline, tight monetary policy, limiting taxes on the wealthy, restraining trade unions through 'labour market flexibility', divesting the state of ownership of public enterprises, a general commitment to small government, removing restrictions on the free flow of goods and capital, and so on.

Although conservatives, including advocates of the Third Way, like to believe that these ideas are the robust conclusions of economics, they are in reality based on the questionable beliefs of a particular school of economics, the neoclassical school. In fact, the leading ideas of the economics establishment have been shown to be highly contestable, both by recent economic history and by formal economic studies. One of the defining features of neoliberal economics is its disdain for the evidence. After all, the superiority of free-market solutions has been demonstrated over and over by the cleverest in the profession. One needs only to open a textbook to see the proofs reduced to diagrams that even the most dull-witted undergraduate can understand. Why bother with the evidence?

This is not the place for a disquisition on the leading propositions of the neoliberal canon,[14] but a few comments on the foremost beliefs illustrate the point. Since the 1970s it has been argued that if a government attempts to push unemployment down too far it will spark a damaging outbreak of inflation, which will defeat the original intent. Despite some initial resistance from unreconstructed Keynesians, there is now almost universal acceptance among economists that there is a 'natural rate of unemployment' and that if the actual rate is pushed below the natural rate inflation will accelerate. Various attempts to estimate the natural rate have shown that, if it exists at all, it is disturbingly unstable. Moreover, as unemployment falls estimates of the natural rate tend to be revised downwards, so that it always seems to be marginally below the level that happens to prevail at the time. One begins to suspect that the purpose of the concept is to absolve government of the responsibility to pursue full employment. In 1995 US economists David Card and Alan Krueger created a sensation by showing that employment growth was higher in those US states that had *rising* minimum wages.[15] This conclusion so flagrantly defied the most basic premise of neo-classical economics—demand for a commodity falls as its price rises—that vigorous attempts were made to discredit it. The attempts failed. Card and Krueger were right because the labour market deals in a 'commodity' that is unlike any other, and raising the price of labour can change the quality and amount of it supplied and the way it is used. Yet economists and business commentators argue daily that rising wages will mean loss of jobs, especially in a 'globally competitive' world.

Another unchallengeable belief of economic orthodoxy is that any restriction on the mobility of capital will harm investment and slow growth. This has been the central argument used to rationalise the insistence by the International Monetary Fund (IMF) that all countries, including those with underdeveloped financial systems, should liberalise their capital markets to allow the free flow of capital. But there is no reason to believe that measures to limit short-term speculative capital flows will harm long-term investment in productive enterprise. Indeed, greater stability in capital markets works in the interest of long-term investors because they need to take fewer precautions against volatility in exchange rates and interest rates. The IMF has been reluctant to admit this possibility, even after its disastrous attempts to deal with the Asian financial crisis of 1998. Its dogmatic approach was vehemently attacked by former chief economist at the World Bank (and subsequent Nobel Prize winner) Joseph Stiglitz, who pointed out that capital markets were liberalised in East Asia not because more savings were needed but because of political pressure from the IMF and the US Treasury.[16] The flood of short-term capital caused the Asian financial crisis to spread and deepen, yet the IMF imposed austerity measures that only made matters worse.

A further shibboleth of modern politics is that governments cannot run businesses profitably: only private owners have the incentives to operate enterprises efficiently. This belief has provided the rationale for the wave of privatisations of public assets throughout the developed and developing worlds since the 1980s and the public–private partnerships that have followed. Sell-offs have been a feature of conservative governments of the left and right, and any reluctance has been met with dire threats from international financial institutions, including the IMF and credit-rating agencies such as Standard and Poors. There are dozens of studies of the relative merits of public and private ownership. The broad conclusion is that, in markets where there is a natural monopoly or where heavy government regulation is necessary to ensure protection of the public, publicly owned enterprises perform at least as well as private ones, and in some cases better. Moreover, it has been shown by a number of studies that the profitability of private companies is higher in countries or regions where governments invest more heavily in the provision of sound infrastructure such as roads, ports and telecommunications. Yet any resistance to further privatisation—let alone calls to re-nationalise some enterprises to undo some of the damage caused by privatisation—is met with howls of outrage, threats of 'capital strikes' and editorials about the evils of a return to 'socialism'.

The final article of faith of neoliberal economics that deserves comment is the belief that everyone benefits from free trade. The textbook theory is elegant, and faith in the benefits of free trade is perhaps the economists' most strongly held belief. Yet it is obvious that the assumptions on which the theory is based—for example, that capital is not mobile and that firms compete on equal terms—are simply not met in practice. For many years, the World Bank claimed that the success of Asia's 'little tigers' was proof of the enormous benefits of free trade. But South Korea, Taiwan and Japan did not practice free trade: they exported vigorously but they also protected their home markets fiercely. The evidence contradicting the World Bank's views was so overwhelming that, in one of its own reports in 1994 and under pressure from Japan, the Bank was forced to concede that pervasive government intervention was an essential part of the industrialisation process that made these countries wealthy.[17] Moreover, even with the abandonment of tariffs, quotas and other non-tariff barriers, there would still not be free trade. There are already a number of legal restrictions on trade that no one challenges: the World Trade Organization rules include bans on trade in products produced by prison and child labour and restrictions on trade in hazardous goods. Calls for 'fair trade' are based on nothing more than a demand for the extension of prohibitions on goods produced in conditions where basic human rights and working conditions are violated or which involve unacceptable damage to the environment.

Despite the accumulation of evidence contradicting the most basic assumptions of the discipline, neoclassical economists cling to these notions as firmly as ever. It is not only the academic economists who propagate these beliefs in lecture halls and professional journals; they are mirrored even more crudely in the prognostications of the 'market economists' we see quoted in the press and on television every day. The fact is that neoclassical economics has been spectacularly unsuccessful at developing a coherent explanation of how national macro-economies work or the forces that drive the global economy. Yet social democratic politicians and academic activists such as Giddens have been unwilling to challenge the neoliberal economic consensus. As a result, while ostensibly rejecting Thatcherism, they have uncritically accepted the economics on which it is based.

Power and equality

There is one political principle to which modern social democracy remains committed and that differentiates it starkly from Thatcherism—greater social equality. Giddens writes, 'One major criterion continually reappears in distinguishing left from right: attitudes towards equality. The Left favours greater equality, while the Right sees society as inevitably hierarchical'.[18] While this

statement is, on the face of it, unexceptional, the Left's understanding of the nature of inequality and therefore the solution
to it has subtly but decisively changed under the influence of
neoliberal social philosophy. The notion of equality has become
ambiguous in the politics of social democracy. In particular, it is
not clear whether advocates of the Third Way believe in greater
equality of opportunity or greater equality of outcomes. Traditionally, the focus has been on equality of outcomes, with the
emphasis on reducing income inequality. The primary response
of social democracy has been the progressive tax system and
public ownership of essential services so that the poor have access
to them. The shift to equality of opportunity is attractive in an
era of apparent public resistance to high taxes since, if disadvantage can be overcome, inequality of outcomes ought to be
reduced. There is, of course, a trap here. If inequality of opportunity is the problem and the problem has been fixed, then
inequality of outcomes simply has to be accepted. However,
equality of opportunity can never be enough if an unacceptable
level of inequality is built into the very structure of the capitalist
economy. If so, there is no escaping the need for redistribution
of outcomes.

To reach this conclusion one needs a social analysis that
identifies the sources of structural inequality, something the advocates of the Third Way assiduously avoid. Instead, the Third Way
has resorted to the idea of 'social exclusion', the term used to
describe lack of opportunity for individuals to develop their
potential. There is no doubt that exclusion is a cause of misery
and disadvantage and has, in some respects, intensified with the
decline of the traditional working class, along with its cultural

norms and social institutions. Structural change and globalisation have seen a large part of the working class shift into the
middle classes and many of the remainder slip into a marginal
existence of long-term unemployment or poorly paid casual jobs
and entrenched poverty. However, instead of powerful social
classes imposing unfair structures that benefit themselves and
leave a segment of the population poor (relatively at least), in the
world view of modern social democracy we must simply accept
that what 'the market' delivers is natural and inevitable. All we
can do is try to modify the impacts by programs that allow
everyone to participate 'equally' in the market.

Such a world view is strongly preferred by social elites because
it has a politically neutralising effect. There is no powerful
oligarchy to point the finger at, only an impersonal system conditioned by the global market that defines the ground rules by
which societies and governments must operate. After two decades
of talk about 'the economy' as an immovable and all-conquering
force, the market has become reified in the public mind, a victory
for the economists' textbooks. The consequence is that misfor-
tune is seen to be a product of the relationship between an
individual and the market, and it is pointless to look for someone
to blame. The solution to disadvantage, therefore, is to fix the
individual rather than the economic and social system. Social
democracy—or at least the Third Way variant of it—has thus
subtly redefined the Left's traditional concern for social justice.
It is now a question not of structural economic disadvantage but
of the politics of life choices. In other words, social justice has
become individualised and divorced from the essential structure

of capitalism at a time when capitalism has reached its most purified form.

The emphasis on equality of opportunity in place of equality
of outcomes has meant that education has become central to the
political program of modern social democracy. Education has
replaced motherhood as the goal no one dares oppose. It is a
universal good and the more we have of it the better off we are.
It can rescue anyone suffering from disadvantage. It is politically
more attractive than motherhood because the state can provide
more and better education simply by allocating more funds
through the budget and training more teachers. 'Education and
training have become the new mantra for social democratic
politicians. Tony Blair famously describes his three main priorities in government as "education, education, education".'[19] The
parallel with the well-known slogan of real estate agents is not
without significance.

It is undeniable that education is important in tackling social
exclusion: the relationship between education and social mobility
is well established. But education cannot be the panacea that
social democrats and conservatives hope for. In short, what is
good for the individual is not necessarily good for society. The
rapid increase in investment in education in recent times has
mostly been a form of 'defensive expenditure' as people attempt
to maintain their position in the employment hierarchy while
everyone around them upgrades their qualifications. There is no
reason to believe that the new emphasis on education will bring
about a more equal or just society, although it may stave off a
worsening of inequality. Indeed, by transferring the blame for
'failure' to the individuals who do not take advantage of the

educational opportunities on offer, the new approach may erode public commitment to greater equality and inclusion.

Information technology has become the other favourite cause of social democratic politicians. Indeed, for some, modern social democracy is characterised as an explicit attempt to reconcile the values of social democracy with the new world of IT. Information technology is considered to have fundamentally reshaped economies and work. For some, it has taken on a sort of mystical power: the 'information society breaks down all forms of hierarchy' and gives everyone access to wealth.[20] The real division today is between the 'information rich' and the 'information poor', and 'knowledge creation' is a priority of the Third Way. The information age will resolve inequality and help 'dissolve the class struggle'.

Oddly, it is the very seriousness with which advocates of the Third Way declare their belief in the transformative power of the information economy that marks them as innocents. Only those unfamiliar with the use of computers can truly fall for the hype of the information economy. Information technology and information are sources of power and influence, and the emergence of the 'information economy' has seen some realignment of economic and political power. But having access to a computer does not give the user access to this power. Adoption of information technology has transformed the work of those at the bottom end of the employment market as much as it has transformed that of those at the top, and has been as much a cause of entrapment as liberation. The fact that computers are useful does not mean we should worship them, yet any number of pundits and politicians have substituted the marketing slogans of infotech for genuine political philosophy. To achieve this new world more quickly, we are told we must transform education systems. By replacing knowledge with information, a specific set of skills is placed above a well-developed critical mind, and this reflects the essential anti-intellectualism of the politics of the Third Way.

Despite all this, the nature of inequality does need to be reconsidered in post-scarcity societies. Such a rethinking must, however, be based on a proper understanding of the implications of abundance rather than on the social philosophy underpinning neoliberal economics. In doing so, it is worthwhile reminding ourselves why social democrats have traditionally been concerned about inequality. The first reason is that inequality is associated with poverty; wealthy societies that have a fairer distribution of income have less poverty, and poverty is unambiguously a bad thing.[21] It is well established that those at the bottom of unequal societies have less access to basic services such as good health care and education and that more unequal societies are more unhealthy societies, even if the average level of income is higher. In addition, inequality is responsible for greater social division, so that the rich and the poor inhabit very different physical and social worlds and have little understanding of the other. It is also associated with differences in political power, so that the wealthy are in a better position to look after themselves at the expense of others. Finally, gross inequality tends to generate envy and resentment on one hand and arrogance and feelings of superiority on the other, all of which lead to a less contented society.

This simple exposition is important because in all the discussion of inequality the reasons why it should be fought are frequently forgotten. But the reasons matter when we consider ways of reducing inequality. Some of the more important reasons why inequality reduces individual and social wellbeing have nothing to do with the distribution of physical wealth as such but are instead related to social and cultural attitudes. A more unequal society is more unhappy, even if most people's incomes are higher than they would be in a more equal society. As discussed in Chapter 2, within a nation a person's actual level of income has less influence on their perceived wellbeing than how their income compares with the incomes of other people, and with their own expectations of the income they would have and the income they should have. In other words, changes in personal attitudes and prevailing social expectations can result in a sharp improvement in individual and social wellbeing, without any change in the physical distribution of a nation's wealth. Even at the high end of the income scale, where more income can have no appreciable impact on standards of living, inequality of incomes can severely affect wellbeing. The very rich are afflicted by feelings of envy and inadequacy. This is because in our societies incomes are a signalling device: they communicate to other people how much the world values what we do, a fact that explains the obscene blow-outs in executive remuneration of the last few years. If there were other markers of social worth, or if people were simply unconcerned with how the world sees them, inequality would matter much less.

In post-scarcity societies, mass poverty no longer exists. Although the figure varies from country to country, 5–15 per cent of populations are significantly or seriously deprived in a material sense. Recognition of this fact leads us to focus directly on poverty itself, rather than on the general distribution of income and wealth in a post-growth society. A change in perceptions about the factors that are important to wellbeing and a devaluation of wealth as the leading indicator of social worth would mean an end to the fixation on the level and distribution of material riches and a much greater emphasis on the factors that do contribute to more rewarding lives. These observations on the features of a post-growth social formation are explored in subsequent chapters, but they should not be taken to mean that we ought to retreat from redistributive policies such as progressive taxation, which ensure fairness in funding public services, including poverty eradication. Policies of this kind will always be needed, no matter how much equality of opportunity is achieved.

6
Work

Rethinking work

In countries where the economic problem has been solved it is no longer necessary or desirable to think of work primarily as a means of material survival. The great majority of people are freed of this constraint, so work can become first and foremost an activity devoted to fulfilling human potential. Since (with important exceptions) questions of payment no longer need to be paramount, in addition to rethinking the structure and purpose of paid work we can dispense with the distinction between paid and unpaid work—including household work, other work at home and work in the community. For the first time, paid and unpaid work can be considered equally valid forms of self-creating activity. In other words, the arrival of abundance allows us to discard ingrained beliefs about work, formed as they were in the Industrial Revolution and before. It is no longer a question of achieving a 'balance' between work and life; it is one of living fully through work, both paid and unpaid.

Traditionally, the Left has been concerned with the relationship between workers and capitalists in the process of production. Struggles over pay and working conditions have provided the inspiration for generations of people on the Left. The contradiction between workers and capitalists has provided the starting point for the analysis of social structure and political change, and even the foundation of a theory of history. Factories, mines and shipyards have been the scenes of hard-fought and often heroic struggles by working people whose very survival has rested in the hands of the owners of capital, and it is for this reason that trade unions have had a crucial role in Left politics. The preoccupation with wages, working conditions and unemployment, and with a welfare state that provides collectively for workers when private markets fail, has meant that Left politics has been above all concerned with activities and relationships in the production sphere. This was consistent with the Left's political analysis of power, since the power of capitalists—individually and collectively—derived from their control over the production process, including employment. This focus on the sphere of production is shared with neoliberalism, although neoliberalism is prone to see power residing in trade unions rather than in ownership of capital and prefers to explain unemployment in terms of the personal failings of the victims rather than the structural features of the system.

In contrast, most of this book is concerned with the sphere of consumption. As discussed in Chapter 3, in the period since the Second World War there has been a dramatic change in the forces that drive society. In the case of capital, modern firms are driven less by competition through cost cutting and more by product differentiation and marketing. In the case of 'workers', questions of identity, social structure and political orientation are now determined more by consumption activities than by production and employment. Previously, social classes, based predominantly on where people found themselves in the production process, were the primary source of personal and social identity. The spread of affluence and the transition to consumer capitalism have meant that identity now has less to do with one's work—where one is placed in the production process—and more to do with one's consumption choices, including the consumption of cultural products. The uniformity of self-definition associated with class identification has been superseded by the apparent differentiation of self associated with the construction of identity through consumption behaviour.

The change in emphasis from the production to the consumption sphere is one shared with postmodern social analysis, except that postmodernism accepts consumption at face value, with little appreciation of its historical purpose or personal significance. It was not 'modernity' that had changed; it was capitalism that had morphed from industrial capitalism into consumer capitalism. Consumer capitalism has now co-opted and transformed those cultural products of society that had hitherto maintained a certain autonomy from the economy. At the systemic level the transition has been prompted, as always, by the imperative of profit, yet the pursuit of profit became increasingly a function of a firm's capacity to surpass rivals through product differentiation, marketing and branding. In short, corporate success depended on a successful appeal to the 'needs' of classes of people whose wealth enabled them to search for a way of expressing themselves through their purchasing behaviour and associated lifestyles. The objective of capital is unchanged and so is its manifestation in corporate power, but the means to it have been utterly transformed. This transition's effect on the definition of self has been as profound as the effect of the transition from feudalism to industrial capitalism, and it is this basic truth that postmodernism has unwittingly grasped.

With the transition to the new form of capitalism, the relationship between ordinary people and corporations has changed dramatically. Where once they responded to the unfair exercise of power by joining industrial trade unions, now they react against perceived exploitation by joining consumer groups and Greenpeace. The failure to recognise that corporate power continues to lie at the centre of social, as well as economic, transformation is the error of both the postmodernists and the advocates of the Third Way. Theorists of postmodernism have forgotten about the economy—the relationships between people and the production and consumption of goods and services— and have had eyes only for processes of cultural change. But, without falling into deterministic Marxist notions of an economic base supporting the political and cultural superstructure, it must be recognised that the processes of cultural change and differentiation are shaped and constrained by the ideological and cultural needs of economic, corporate and, above all, marketing organisations and systems. Individuals cannot be constituted outside of their institutions. In the case of the 'lifestyle politics' of the

Third Way, its advocates fail to understand and react to the way corporations, through their marketers, have seized on and captured the yearning people have for authenticity, attributing 'autonomy' to people who remain captive in an entirely new way.

What does all of this mean for our understanding of work? I have argued that the principal contradictions of modern life lie not in the sphere of production but in the sphere of consumption. The arrival of the age of abundance for the first time provides the possibility of the liberation of work. Transcending the primacy of the growth motive creates the potential and opportunity to restructure work, so that it finally becomes centred on creating the worker rather than the product of work. While abundance provides for the liberation *of* work it should not be taken to mean liberation *from* work, since work is the means to human fulfilment and the expression of creativity.[1] The extent to which this liberation can occur depends on many factors, only some of which can be explored in this chapter. They include the structure of the labour market as well as various influences beyond the labour market. Moreover, it must be acknowledged that, although large numbers of workers labour in occupations that already allow for a certain amount of creativity, there are others, particularly in less-skilled occupations (check-out operators, building labourers, data clerks, and so on), where alienation and drudgery remain hard to avoid. The transformation of these jobs is yet to be done, but their continued existence should not prevent us from seeing that the liberation of work is now possible for the majority of the population.

We should, however, caution ourselves against moving to the other extreme. The archetype of the new flexible, mobile

worker—the 'symbolic analyst', or 'bourgeois bohemian'[2]—
provides no model for the future. Robert Reich suggests that these
'mind workers', who make up around one-fifth of the workforce,
can sell their services anywhere and are happy to do so. But we
should not mistake mobility for freedom. The cosmopolitan elite
is just as prone to manufacturing their identities through the
symbols of consumption as everyone else; indeed, they are more
prone because they are more likely to have uprooted themselves
from communities that act as a counterweight to the free-floating
identity so beloved of the marketers. Cosmopolitans in fact
commodify culture, so that it can be consumed rather than experienced. As Thompson and Tambyah argue:

> Cosmopolitans actively consume cultural differences in a
> reflexive, intellectualizing manner, whereas locals remain
> content in their parochial ways of life . . . Cosmopolitanism
> is . . . a style of consumption that creates and maintains
> status distinctions between high-cultural-capital consumers
> and low-cultural-capital consumers.[3]

Travel and detachment are seen as being at the core of identities
marked by a sophisticated global outlook, but they are identities
that frequently suppress the anguish of voluntary homelessness.

Reconsideration of work has a particular resonance for young
people. Radical changes in the nature of the labour market—the
death of career, the decline of standard hours and the rise of casu-
alisation—have already meant that young people are less
preoccupied than their parents with security and long-term plans
and more determined to find working arrangements that offer
them fulfilment and personal growth. At least, this is true for

those with the education to allow some meaningful choice. Some European analysts go further and apply the idea to the workforce in general. In the words of Oskar Negt, 'A distancing from work, a critical evaluation of whether one's work is really a worthwhile activity, has taken hold on the consciousness of broad masses of the population'.[4] This is an undoubted trend, reflecting both the liberation that abundance permits and, perversely, the sundering of old ties and obligations in the employment relationship introduced by neoliberal governments and corporations seeking flexibility. While Negt's observation holds true across large cohorts of youths and young adults, its general application awaits more radical and deliberate social change.

Nevertheless, in a post-scarcity world work can be liberated from the bonds of wage and salary payment, so that it can be considered a creative self-realising activity. Moreover, we can finally break down the barriers between paid employment and work in the household and the community. Rebalancing of paid and unpaid work is an essential component of this rethinking, but its implications go much further. As Gorz has written:

> Reducing working hours will not have a liberating effect, and will not change society, if it merely serves to redistribute work and reduce unemployment . . . It requires a *politics of time* which embraces the reshaping of the urban and natural environment, cultural politics, education and training, and reshapes the social services and public amenities in such a way as to create more scope for self-managed activities, mutual aid, voluntary co-operation and production for one's own use.[5]

The new labour market

At a public meeting in a regional city a few years ago, 200 people gathered to hear a lecture on economic growth and the meaning of progress. During the discussion time many people commented on the personal and social troubles caused by widespread unemployment. Then one man stood up and said that three years previously he had lost his job because of an industrial accident. Some months later when he had recovered, he began looking for work but, despite his sustained efforts, could find none. After a year or so he lapsed into despair and stared suicide in the face. Then one day he woke up and decided to look at his situation another way. Now, he told the audience, he has three jobs. They are all voluntary and, although he does not have much money, he has never felt so fulfilled and happy.

In the economics textbooks, work is characterised by its 'disutility', the suffering associated with the act of labour; we engage in work activity each day for only one purpose, to earn income to enable us to buy consumer goods. The theory is based on the view that we would all prefer to be idle, whiling away our lives in leisure pursuits, but our consumption demands compel us to go out and work.[6] The textbook theory of wages is built on this foundation. While employers' demand for labour depends on how much value a worker can add to output in a day, workers supply their labour to the market up to the point where the pain from an extra hour of work exceeds the pleasure they receive from the extra wages. Thus, in this view of the world workers are free to decide how much they will work and how much they will enjoy leisure, given the wage they can earn with their level of skill.

Consequently, restrictions on the ability of individual workers to supply their labour or on the ability of employers to offer work to anyone at any wage are not only restrictions on basic rights but are economically inefficient. To avoid such restrictions, power must be dissipated by vigorous competition between employers and unfettered competition between workers, who must be free to choose where and how much they work.

The Left has had a very different understanding of how workers fit into the labour market—one in which power is naturally in the hands of employers. In the era of industrial capitalism the nature of the labour process and the relationship between workers and employers meant that work, instead of being a free expression of creative capacities, became alienating, so that workers' capacities were constrained and crippled. Moreover, the fruits of their labour were appropriated for the benefit of others. Workers could sometimes combine into trade unions in order to counterbalance the power of capital by withholding their labour or influencing governments to impose laws that improve wages and conditions. But, in the end, capital always had the whip hand.

The Left's analysis is unquestionably closer to the truth. Work, paid or otherwise, is inseparable from living a full and rewarding life. Although some ascetics seek their inner selves through long periods of meditative retreat, for most people purposeful activity is the means to fulfilment. Among the many who have studied the role of work, Jahoda argues that employment provides five categories of psychological experience that are vital to well-being—time structure, social contact, collective effort or purpose, social identity or status, and regular activity.[7] Most of all, and notwithstanding the role of consumption in modern identity

formation, work continues to provide a sense of personal identity, and it for this reason above all that in wealthy societies the
wellbeing of workers declines so dramatically when they become
unemployed. While the ostensible purpose of employment is to
earn income in order to consume, in modern times the unemployed suffer most not from material deprivation but from the
corrosive psychological impacts of exclusion from meaningful
activity and the concomitant absence of time structure, idleness,
impoverishment of social experience, and loss of social status.
Jahoda comments on how unemployment eats away at one's sense
of self: 'Because of widespread consensus in public life about the
social status assigned to varying jobs, people tend to adopt this
assignation as one clear element in defining themselves to themselves and are reluctant to dispense with this support for their
personal identity'.[8]

While it is politically convenient for conservative politicians
and populist demagogues to attack the unemployed for their lazi-
ness and their willingness to sponge on society, in fact few people
are equipped to sustain their mental health when they have no
way of filling their day in a structured and purposeful way. This
is why so many men enter a period of deep malaise, often leading
to illness and death, when they retire. Rotary clubs owe their existence to this psychological fact.

Few jobs are so lacking in psychological reward as to render
prolonged unemployment preferable. How, then, do we explain
the fact that some people discover that their lives are improved
by being made unemployed?[9] Haworth reports a study of a small
group of people who, on becoming redundant, experienced
material deprivation but no psychological loss. Each of these

unemployed workers could distinguish between employment and meaningful work and 'the majority indicated the importance of having values that gave direction to life including political, religious and personal development beliefs'.[10] The study showed that these people obtained the psychological benefits of employment by other means. Their new activities allowed them to structure their time and share experience outside the home (and in some cases inside the home as well). They had 'transcending' goals and purposes, and many derived status and identity from new activities such as voluntary work. These people are the exceptions that prove the rule about the psychological damage of unemployment: they demonstrate that purposeful work, rather than paid employment, provides the rewards people most crave. Those who benefit from redundancy or retirement benefit not because they are freed to indulge in idleness but because they are freed from one form of activity to take up another that they find more rewarding. Unlike the man whose story opens this section, these people are usually able to sustain a reasonable level of consumption once their payments stop, but it is remarkable how many of them report that the decline in material rewards has meant no great loss of life satisfaction.

In the 1960s it was widely believed that within decades we would witness a transition from a life of work to a life of leisure. Extrapolating from the historical decline in working hours, and noting the apparently unlimited labour-saving properties of technological progress, commentators foreshadowed societies in which the populace would indulge in a life of lotus-eating relieved of the drudgery of work. These forecasts could not have been more inaccurate. Writing in *Fortune* magazine in 1994, William

Bridges summed up the feeling: 'We used to read predictions that by the year 2000 everyone would work 30-hour weeks, and the rest would be leisure. But as we approach 2000 it seems more likely that half of us will be working 60-hour weeks and the rest of us will be unemployed. What's wrong?'[11]

In the early 1980s working hours for full-time employees in the West stopped their historical decline and, contrary to expectations, began to increase, especially in the Anglophone countries. There is much popular comment on the phenomenon of overwork and 'time stress'. The pressure on work time has occupied many analysts, with some wondering whether work patterns in the United States and Europe were mimicking the legendary overwork of Japan's 'salarymen' and factory workers. It is a vision few have welcomed. Acute observer Gavan McCormack has noted that nowhere is the crippling effect of modern work more apparent than in Japan, where working hours are much longer than in other rich countries. In the car industry, Japanese workers put in an average of 2275 hours each year, 33 per cent more than their counterparts in Europe.[12] A 55-hour week is common and fewer than 20 per cent of employees enjoy a two-day weekend. Despite Japan's wealth, the pressure to work longer and harder has intensified in the last two decades. Even employers have acknowledged the corrosive effect of such a 'work ethic': the chairman of Sony Corporation, Moria Akio, wrote that Japan is 'in desperate need of a new philosophy of management, a new paradigm for competitiveness, a new sense of self'. The key to this, he said, is shorter working hours, something that most Japanese workers want.[13]

Overwork among full-time employees was not the only startling new feature of the labour market and the nature of work to emerge in the 1980s and 1990s. The widespread unemployment that grew out of the recession of the early to mid-1970s persisted, leading to the creation of a substantial underclass of long-term unemployed, with serious social ramifications. Gorz refers to the 'post-industrial proletariat', made up of the unemployed, the occasionally employed and those in precarious casual or part-time work,[14] and suggests that they make up 40–50 per cent of the workforce in Western European countries. We must, however, distinguish between people who are on the margins of the labour force and desire, with varying degrees of desperation, full-time work in order to attain a decent standard of living and people in a wide variety of circumstances who are not motivated to join the labour force in the traditional way. In Europe more than half of part-time workers have deliberately sought their working arrangements.[15] Among women employees, 42 per cent would prefer to work fewer hours; 54 per cent of male employees would prefer to work fewer hours, one-third of them wanting to work more than five hours less.[16] Young people, in particular, often spend years moving in and out of the workforce while they pursue a range of other 'projects', sometimes supported by casual work or by payments from the state or their parents or partners, but often living without the need for substantial incomes. These 'workers' feel no compulsion to define themselves or find their life course through paid employment; instead, they seek autonomy through a range of other, unpaid, activities, a choice permitted by social arrangements in the era of abundance. This is a far-reaching but little acknowledged social transformation, for it reflects not only the fact that the 'economic problem' has been solved but that the even harder nut of economic rationality has also been cracked. In his 1930 essay 'Economic Possibilities for our Grandchildren', Keynes wondered whether the nut could be cracked at all:

> Thus we have been expressly evolved by nature—with all of our impulses and deepest instincts—for the purpose of solving the economic problem . . . Yet I think with dread of the readjustment of the habits and instincts of the ordinary man, bred into him for countless generations, which he may be asked to discard within a few decades.[17]

Keynes's concern about the inbred work habits of the ordinary man is a nice counterpoint to the presumption of modern economics texts that the basic instinct of *homo economicus* is sloth. But Keynes could not have seen how abundance would transform the psychology of ordinary people. Perhaps that is because he used as his marker of the future the example set by the wives of the well-to-do, 'unfortunate women . . . who have been deprived by their wealth of their traditional occupations—who cannot find it sufficiently amusing . . . to cook and clean and mend, yet are quite unable to find anything more amusing'.[18] Freud's work also suffered from the assumption that bourgeois women of the turn of the century constituted a representative sample.

Thus the creation of large numbers of part-time and casual jobs has been a result partly of the demand for part-time jobs, especially from women workers entering the labour force, and a result partly of the supply of part-time jobs by employers seeking greater flexibility of employment. The effect on people's lives has been profound, but it has been a double-edged sword. For many workers, part-time work suits their circumstances perfectly, while others, anxious for full-time work, must subsist on half or less of what they require.

Whatever the effect on people's lives, the old model of full-time male breadwinners is now redundant. In general, only about one-third of workers work a 'standard' week of around 40 hours; another third work substantially more, and the remainder work part time or not at all.[19] Some analysts have seen only the downside of the new flexible workplaces. The sharp increase in mobility and outsourcing has weakened the forces that previously bound employees to their workplaces. In his influential book *The Corrosion of Character*, Richard Sennett observes that a young American with two years of college education can expect to change jobs eleven times in a 40-year working life and to retrain at least three times.[20] He reflects on the corporate motto 'No long term' and quotes an executive talking about 'the contingent worker' and companies where 'jobs' are being replaced by 'projects' and 'fields of work'. Sennett argues that we need long-term relationships in order to develop trust, and that the sense of place associated with familiar workplaces is fundamental to being emotionally rooted. Change can be stimulating, but too much of it leaves us floating and uncertain. Yet this is precisely what suits modern capitalism—the imperatives of growth make everything expendable and the capriciousness of consumer tastes requires businesses to be ever more light-footed. Sennett comments thus on the psychological implications of the new world of work: 'Detachment and superficial cooperativeness are better armor for dealing with current realities than behavior based on values of loyalty and service'.[21]

Arguably, it is safer to try to put down emotional roots by creating a personal 'lifestyle' through the consumption decisions over which one has total control, rather than through a job for which there is no long term. The central feature of modern life is the rise of individualisation, the process in which people, no longer defined and constrained by social categories of class, status and gender, must 'write their own biographies'. But although we are freed from the constraints of the past—constraints that, while limiting, also provided a sense of security and of knowledge of who we are and where we fit—the new labour market conspires against us in our efforts to find a course through life. As Sennett observes, 'How can a human being develop a narrative of identity and life history in a society composed of episodes and fragments?'[22]

The contradictory nature of changes in the labour market is captured in the history of the idea of a career. It is often said that women today have difficulty balancing their home lives with their careers. But what is this idea of a career? At one level it is a progression up a well-defined path in a profession or, less formally perhaps, the continuing acquisition of skills and experience that makes someone a more productive and valuable worker. Sennett argues that the idea of pursuing a 'career'—a word that originally meant a road for carriages and came to mean 'a lifelong channel for one's economic pursuits'[23]—emerged in the early part of the 20th century as a means of countering the danger of a life of aimlessness, an 'antidote to personal failure'.

My father, a 'career' public servant, lived in an era when men acquired status and a place in the social order by demonstrating the qualities of reliability, stoicism and loyalty. Those who put these qualities above others were rewarded. The need for the security of a career owed a great deal to the depredations of the Great Depression. If their own fathers had not been thrown out of work and their families forced onto the breadline, then certainly their neighbours' had been. But the career, then as now, was frequently a trap, a cocoon of security and social sanction that prevented men from spreading their wings and seeking out the niche in the world that would allow them to realise their potential. They were frustrated. The fact is that, even for those who successfully work their way to the top of their chosen career path over 40 years, the bulk of the time is spent treading water, engaged in activities that do not in any way contribute to their professional capabilities or personal advancement.

The superabundance of modern capitalism has liberated people from the need to cling to a career path. One has to ask, then, why women worry about threats to a career. Admittedly, there are times in a career that are more important than others for making progress, but for the most part those who make early progress end up spending longer periods marking time later on. Young people are increasingly replacing the idea of a career with the notion of a life narrative,[24] a transition consistent with the era of individualisation. Certainly, the idea of autonomously living out one's life story has more appeal than pursuing a career whose indicators of success are defined by some impersonal reference group motivated by self-validation. Yet society conspires against the brave, for the career is, above all, an insurance policy against failure. In a society of winners and losers, most people lose. In fact, even the winners lose. While there appears to be no way back from having your 'career destroyed', rewriting your life narrative allows you to confront your failures, integrate them into the story, and move on. Abandoning the idea of a career is in fact a process of self-liberation, an act of taking control of your life. In a post-scarcity society, one can fail in one's career but succeed as a man or a woman.

The wholesale transformation of labour markets in the late 20th century has been quite properly criticised by the Left for robbing many segments of the workforce of security, but it has also opened up enormous opportunities to go beyond the deadening relationships of the past. Labour market changes have not reflected only the wishes of employers: some workers have been able to renegotiate the way they work so as to suit their own preferences and family needs. Increasing numbers of people want to have more control over their work, especially their working time. The enormous growth of part-time work has perfectly suited large numbers of workers, especially students and women with children. Many others have been able to work as independent contractors or consultants. Although it is more risky, this way of working offers a degree of flexibility and autonomy, which explains why some workers who are made redundant subsequently see it as the best thing that could have happened to them.

In praise of housework

One of the unfortunate consequences of the success of the women's movement has been the devaluation of household work. While for many women a lifetime of 'home duties' meant a lifetime of boredom and an enormous waste of latent talent, at least before the 1970s being a housewife had recognised social status. To be sure, it was a social status *sui generis*, outside the hierarchy of professions and trades, but it was universally acknowledged and understood. The more recent disparagement of 'home duties' was coupled with the emerging sense that women who stayed at home, even to raise young children, were committing themselves to activities of no value. But however much that status might have been constructed by males for the benefit of males, we must ask whether the solution was to denigrate and disparage the activity rather than transform it. For many women, what drove them into the labour market in huge numbers in the 1970s and 1980s (mostly into part-time work) was as much the desire to avoid being left in a role that society had suddenly decided was of no value as the lure of financial independence and a career. The fate of those who refused, even temporarily, was to be characterised as talentless drudges or passive victims of patriarchy.

The 1990s saw the eruption of deep-seated dissatisfaction with this state of affairs. After all, the housework still had to be done, and neither men, technology nor the market seemed able or willing to take over the task. There was a brief celebration of the Superwoman who successfully juggled career, children and housework, but that has been superseded by some profound questioning of the desirability of the whole project. On one hand, serious questions have been raised about the capacity of paid child-care workers to provide the love and security that young children need. The gnawing guilt of mothers (and some fathers) has been compounded by a new body of research documenting the psychological and developmental disadvantages of children consigned too early to long-day care. On the other hand, the sheen of the male world of work—the career, the status and the independence—became decidedly tarnished. As I have argued, these doubts received one of their strongest expressions in Germaine Greer's *The Whole Woman*, in which the seminal voice of anarcho-feminism maintained that women had accepted equality in place of liberation. Equality allowed women to unlock the cage only to find themselves in the bigger cage that men too laboured in. For Greer, the problem had become not just patriarchy, but patriarchy conditioned by the global system of corporate and consumer capitalism. If we take the patriarchy out of capitalism we are still left with capitalism and all its superficiality, materialism and exploitation of the Third World.

And still the housework remained to be done. A new appreciation of its value is emerging, along with that of its less-disparaged partner, voluntary work in the community. Household work is the material foundation of a living environment that is healthy, comfortable, supportive, nurturing and loving. We allocate time to the various tasks—cooking, cleaning, washing, child care, gardening, shopping, home maintenance, and so on—roughly according to how much each contributes to our own and our household's wellbeing. In fact, household work contributes enormously to our physical comfort and emotional contentment. In the right circumstances, doing household work can be one of the most rewarding ways for people to spend time nurturing themselves and their families. This helps explain why, despite major advances in household technology that have reduced the time and effort people need to devote to many tasks (and the availability of commercial services for those who can afford them), time-use surveys show that households in Western countries today devote as many hours a week to household work as they did in the 1950s.[25]

People who remember life in the 1950s might recall their mothers hauling sopping clothes from the washing machine to the hand-operated wringer, clothes they may have made themselves. They might remember their fathers cutting the grass with a push mower and chopping wood or hauling coal to heat the house. There were no dishwashing machines, microwave ovens, steam irons or clothes driers, and pre-prepared foods were confined to canned fruit, fish and meat. Despite the 1970s and 1980s disparagement of housework and those who did it, people's unwillingness to reduce the amount of housework when the opportunity arose is telling. Some have attributed this to demands for higher standards of cleanliness, better quality meals, and so on. Advertisers have promoted this creep in standards, urging us to have floors we can eat off and trying to frighten us with fears of hidden germs. But perhaps the main reason that time devoted to household work has not declined is the obvious one: people like to do it. Or at least they like to have the sort of family and home life that housework provides. While the performing of housework can be a chore, it can also be satisfying. The act itself, as well as its outcome, contributes to our wellbeing.

Because housework contributes to a warm, loving and nurturing home environment, we are mistaken to think of it merely as an activity that produces 'household goods and services'. There is a strong current of thought, particularly in the feminist movement and spreading into official thinking, that household activities should be considered in the same way as paid work outside the home. On this basis demands are made for women to be paid for the work they do in the household. Although this is an understandable response to the historical trivialisation of women's work, there are grave dangers in such a proposal. In this view, household work is characterised as the process of production of household goods and services that are consumed by members of the household. The Genuine Progress Indicator described in Chapter 2 accounts for household work in this way. But, while the GPI is a useful device for pointing to the narrowness of official thinking about progress and to the influence of androcentric notions of value, the commodification of household work—like the commodification of the natural environment—serves to change the work's character and devalue it.

Characterising housework as 'work' that happens to be performed in the home is a misguided attempt to induce greater equality between the work of women and men. It is a short step from paid housework to the full representation of domestic relationships in economic terms, as in the perverse world of neoliberal economics analysed in the seventies by Gary Becker, the Chicago economist par excellence. In an article published in one of the profession's most prestigious journals,[26] Becker defined marriage as an arrangement to secure the mutual benefit of exchange between two agents of different endowments. In other words, people marry in order to more efficiently produce 'household commodities', including 'the quality of meals, the quality and quantity of children, prestige, recreation, companionship, love, and health status'. The marriage decision is therefore based on quantifiable costs and benefits. The gain from marriage has to be balanced against the costs, including legal fees and the costs of searching for a mate, to determine whether marriage is worthwhile.

Becker went on to analyse the effect of 'love and caring' on the nature of the 'equilibrium in the marriage market'. He defined love as 'a non-marketable household commodity', noting that more love between potential partners increases the amount of caring and that this in turn reduces the costs of 'policing' the marriage. Policing is needed 'in any partnership or corporation' because it 'reduces the probability that a mate shirks duties or appropriates more output than is mandated by the equilibrium in the marriage market'. After pages of differential calculus, Becker reached a triumphant conclusion: since love produces more efficient marriages, 'love and caring between two persons increase their chances of being married to each other'. What Becker's wife thought about this analysis is not recorded, but the Royal Swedish Academy of Sciences was sufficiently impressed to award him the Nobel Prize for Economics in 1992.

This is the path down which proposals to turn housework into a paid activity inevitably go. The commodification of household work brings the value system of neoliberal economics into the realm where *homo economicus* is least welcome. Not only are 'goods and services' such as cooked meals and clean clothes turned into marketable commodities; even the love of a parent for a child must succumb. It is then only a matter of economic calculation to decide whether or not to contract out the range of services provided within the home—including care of infants and even, as Gorz suggests, the processes of conception, gestation and birth themselves though exogenesis, growing the foetus in vitro to the point of 'birth'.[27]

It is, of course, important to avoid glamorising housework. It can turn into drudgery, but the most common cause of this is the unfair distribution of it and the failure of those who benefit from it to appreciate its meaning—that failure itself often being a product of patriarchy. Although the distribution of housework remains unequal, it is less unequal than it was 30 years ago. Surely the answer is not the transformation of the home into a factory for producing household goods and services and the inevitable imposition of economic rationality, but the democratisation of the household. In a democratic household, differentiation can be consistent with equality. In such a household, those who perform the household work are already paid, in the sense that they have an equal right to the income that comes into the household from the person or people working outside the home for pay. The difference between the democratic household and the commod-ified household is the difference between the warm home and the cold home.

Similar comments could be made about the commodification of voluntary work in the community. The transformation of charities into businesses that deliver government services under contract changes them at their heart. The application of economic rationality to community work destroys its spirit and thus its purpose.

Work in a post-growth world

The shift to self-employment, or 'ownwork',[28] and the spread of part-time work are laying the foundation for a post-growth society. While capitalist enterprises are driven by the need to make profits and expand, people who work for themselves or in small self-directed groups do not of necessity operate under the same compulsions. Even some capitalist enterprises are showing a change in organisational goals, recognising that providing a congenial and flexible workplace for their employees can be viable, although in the end the interests of shareholders rather than employees will always prevail. The entry of women into the labour force and the feminisation of many professions previously reserved for men provide an excellent opportunity to change the nature of work and attitudes to it, although progress in this regard has generally been disappointing, with women too often adopting male approaches to work.

In response to the epidemic of overwork, commentators often suggest that we should not live to work but work to live. Ironically, the idea of working to live is precisely the model that informs neoliberal economics texts, where work has an instrumental function, one that allows for achievement of the real purpose of life—enjoyment of time away from work. (We need to remember that 'work' here encompasses all purposive activity, paid and unpaid.) An essential feature of a post-growth society, perhaps its defining feature, is the dissolution of the boundary between 'work' and 'life', so that work becomes life. In an era of abundance we should not be confronted with the problem of work–life balance: we should revel in the merging of the two. A century ago most workers over a lifetime spent roughly 70 per cent of their waking hours at work. For young people today, the combination of more years in education and longer retirement, coupled with shorter working hours, sabbaticals and breaks for other pursuits, means they will spend around 25 per cent of their waking lives working for pay. They will not spend the other 75 per cent idle; instead, they will pursue a proliferation of projects that will provide discrete chapters and narrative threads for their life biographies.

Andre Gorz also takes a longer view, imagining a society in which, after a 200-year interregnum, people can once again own their own time, time that was taken away by the world of commerce and wage labour. This applies to both work time and leisure time. In the last several decades commerce has systematically attempted to colonise the 'free time' of workers and turn it to consumptive purposes. Leisure activities increasingly require an entrance fee or a pay-TV subscription. Tradition-rich sporting teams have been bought up and repackaged. Urging the Left to 'seize the emancipatory potential of post-industrial civilization', Gorz writes that the objectives must be:

> To force capital . . . to leave the savings of working time at the free disposal of a society in which economically rational activities can no longer be preponderant; to fight for the expansion of spaces of autonomy in which economic purposes and commodity logic no longer prevail; and to render . . . development favourable to the reappropriation by individuals of time, of their environment, of their model of consumption and their mode of social cooperation . . . [29]

In an observation reminiscent of the discussion of Keynes's doubts about the psychological aptitude of ordinary people to take the opportunity when it is presented, Gorz adds, 'It will be objected, no doubt, that all this presupposes the desire and the capacity on the part of individuals to reappropriate time. But this is precisely the nature of the cultural change that is currently under way'.

Quite so. The culture of long hours has been encouraged by pressures from business and its appeal is enhanced by the fear of redundancy, but the greater part of the culture of long hours is entirely voluntary. With the exception of an important group of workers in less-skilled occupations, people have a choice over their jobs. It is the cultural rather than the economic power of capital that convinces them they must work longer and harder: they do so because of their belief about how much income they need in order to maintain an acceptable lifestyle and because income and job status remain central to social status. In other words, people have become habituated to high levels of income to sustain their sense of worth. Globalisation, as a cultural phenomenon, has spread and intensified the habit. But if in a post-growth social formation our sense of personal identity is allowed to flourish through free expression of our creative potential, the culture of overwork will fall away.

7

Environment

The voraciousness of growth

It is commonplace to observe that the current pattern of material consumption is environmentally unsustainable. We hear statements along the lines that if everyone in the world were to consume as much as the average consumer in the rich countries we would require four planets the size of Earth. For the most part, the general public's reaction to declarations by scientists and environmental activists that the expansion of the economy cannot be sustained physically is one of short-lived alarm followed by passivity, as if the problems are too overwhelming to dwell on. The implication of the unsustainability of material consumption levels—that we may need to transform our ways of living—challenges some of the most fundamental beliefs about how we live and how the future will unfold, a world view in which continued growth is assumed. The political aspirations of environmentalism are hamstrung by growth fetishism: however much people may agree that we need to change our lifestyles so that we tread more lightly on Earth, when put to the test most people go cold. The attachments appear too strong. In contrast, socialist revolutionaries had an easier task because they promised better material living standards for the mass of ordinary people.

Economists and business representatives respond to the claim that economic growth is unsustainable with the claim that technology will save the day. This is an appealing argument because it permits a reconciliation of the conflict between our altruistic desire to see a more healthy environment and our self-centred desire to consume more. It is true that technological change has in some instances sharply reduced the volume of resources needed to produce certain goods and services. Silicon fibres substitute for copper wires; compared with 30 years ago, much less aluminium is now used to make a can; and recycling has had a major impact on the use of virgin materials in paper making. But the fact remains that the growth of the world's economies each year calls for greater volumes of natural resources and results in ever-growing volumes of waste. Whenever growth in the use of a resource (such as water, land or fertilisers) or the volume of a waste generated (such as greenhouse gases or toxic wastes) is examined, it becomes apparent that the future depends on the extent to which technological change and, in some cases, changing patterns of consumption can counter the effects of relentless economic growth. Economic growth is voracious, constantly eroding the temporary economies in resource use and waste generation that technological advance allows. According to one study of the United States, Japan and three European countries, the total output of wastes and pollutants increased by 28 per cent between 1975 and 1996, despite substantial efficiency gains in the use of materials.[1] Barring a prolonged world depression, global GDP will increase nearly threefold over the next 50 years. This means that resource consumption will increase nearly threefold unless technological change can offset it or consumption patterns change markedly so that they are less intensive in terms of the use of raw materials. But even to keep the impact of economic activity on Earth at its current destructive level, technological advance will have to reduce resource use per unit of output to but a quarter of the current levels.

The scale of the human impact on Earth is immense. Herman Daly has pointed out that humans currently appropriate 40 per cent of the net product of Earth's land-based photosynthesis.[2] In other words, humans use up 40 per cent of Earth's plant growth. Seventy years ago we used up only 10 per cent and, if current rates of conversion of land continue, in 35 years we will consume 80 per cent. Daly observes that this represents a transition from a world that was relatively empty of human activity to one that is full—overfull. We exploit half the usable fresh water in the world, and we have even disturbed the great chemical cycles that define Earth as a system, those of carbon, nitrogen and phosphorus.[3] For example, Earth's stocks of carbon have over the millennia been cycled through the atmosphere (in the form of carbon dioxide), the surface of the land (in vegetation), underground (as fossil fuels), and in the oceans (as life forms and carbon dioxide). By burning fossil fuels mined from carbon stored safely underground for aeons, thereby putting extra carbon dioxide into the atmosphere, we have disrupted the entire climate system of Earth, with potentially catastrophic consequences.

Researchers have compared humans' annual demand for resources with the area of land needed to generate the required resources and absorb the wastes, including the total area globally available for growing crops, grazing animals, harvesting timber, accommodating infrastructure, marine fishing, and absorption of carbon dioxide produced by burning fossil fuels.[4] They calculated that in 1961 human demand for resources was about 70 per cent of Earth's ability to regenerate; by the 1980s demand had grown to equal the annual supply of resources, and by the end of the 1990s it exceeded by 20 per cent Earth's capacity to sustain consumption. 'It takes the biosphere, therefore, at least a year and three months to renew what humanity uses in a single year', so that humanity is now eating its capital, Earth's natural capital.[5] Every economics student knows that to maintain living standards over time a person must live off the interest on their capital and that to improve living standards they must accumulate more capital. Whether or not the figures are precise, the trend is unquestionable.

Economic growth—the product of population growth and growth in consumption per person—is insistently propelling this process of environmental decline. Building on a mass of scientific analysis, the modern environment movement has posed the most fundamental challenge, not just to our management of Earth's resources but to the growth project itself. It has forced us to ask whether we can have continued economic growth while protecting the resource base of human life and the ecological systems that sustain us. Alarming as this may appear, the evidence shows that the economic losses associated with even the more far-reaching measures are generally small and transitory. The reason for this is simple. Investment propels growth. Market economies work by allocating the volume of capital to the investment opportunities available, and an environmental restriction that reduces the profitability of one type of investment will result in the investment flowing to another area where an economic return, while perhaps a little lower, is still achievable. Even if whole industries are shut down, the economy-wide effects are usually small: capital finds new areas to invest in. Of course, significant structural adjustment costs can be incurred if fixed investments (in buildings, machinery, and so on) cannot be adapted to new uses. The greatest costs are imposed on the workers who find themselves redundant and unable to find similar work in the area where they live. At times, society has quite rightly felt an obligation to provide the support needed for retraining, relocation, and development of new industries.

The cost of protecting the environment is low. Studies consistently demonstrate that countries with tighter environmental regulations do not show any signs of economic losses. In a comprehensive review the OECD concluded, 'There is no evidence that high or relatively high environmental standards have had a systematic negative impact on competitiveness of firms, industries or economies'.[6] Indeed, there is good evidence that those who move first on environmental regulation can enjoy significant economic advantages. It is well known that in the 1970s Germany managed to capture the lion's share of the huge world market in pollution-control equipment because it adopted much tougher restrictions on domestic pollution than the rest of the world. When the German government adopted these aggressive controls, industry was outraged, and any number of economists and financial journalists were wheeled out to predict economic ruin. Today, British officials publicly express regret that they bowed to industry and allowed Germany to take the lead, because it is now difficult to dislodge German pollution-control firms from markets throughout the world.

A celebrated example of how, after predictions of ruin, industry can adapt quickly and effectively to tight environmental standards is provided by US power stations when they were confronted with limits imposed on their sulphur emissions. A unique system of 'cap and trade' restricted the amount of sulphur dioxide the industry could emit but allowed the participating electricity utilities to trade emission permits with each other. The price of permits in the marketplace reflects the cost to industry of meeting the environmental regulation. At the start of the scheme in 1990, industry predicted that the cost of a permit to pollute would be crippling, reaching up to $1000 for each ton of sulphur dioxide. The government was more sanguine but still estimated high prices for permits. Once the system got under way, however, prices peaked at $212 a ton and since then have mostly hovered around $120.[7] Business had simply found better ways of cutting their sulphur dioxide emissions, thereby sharply reducing demand for permits and driving down the 'marginal cost of abatement'. As for aggregate costs, when the legislation came into force in 1990, industry lobbyists claimed the costs would be between $3 billion and $7 billion a year, rising to between $7 billion and $25 billion by the year 2000. But as the data came in the estimates of the long-term costs fell from $1.8 billion initially to

$1 billion a year. Not only were the costs of meeting the regulation one-fifth to one-tenth of those predicted, the electricity utilities actually reduced their sulphur emissions by 30 per cent below the level required by law.

The point here is that, while there is often a trade-off between growth and the environment, the costs to the economy are generally of little significance and often end up producing benefits in the longer term. But our business and political leaders are so fearful of anything with the potential to affect the growth rate that even a very small price is too much to pay—even as an insurance policy for the long-term survival of capitalist expansion. It is an irony that environmentalists generally have more faith in the market system's ability to find a way to accommodate environmental restrictions than the upholders of free markets in the business press and conservative parties. Nevertheless, despite the overwhelming evidence of the minimal economic costs of environmental protection and the obvious longer term economic advantages, claims that environmental laws will reduce growth continue to have almost magical power over political decision makers.

Nowhere is the political and ideological force of growth fetishism more apparent that in the long, tortuous debate over how to tackle global warming. Here we are confronted by the most frightening threat to the future of the world, set out with chilling understatement in the various reports of the UN's Intergovernmental Panel on Climate Change (IPCC). By the end of the century we could see Earth's mean temperature rise by 6 degrees centigrade. (At the height of the last Ice Age, when New York was several metres under ice, Earth's mean temperature was only 5 degrees cooler than it is now.) Sea-level rise of nearly 1 metre by the end of the century (the upper estimate of the IPCC), due mainly to thermal expansion of the oceans, would see Bangladesh lose 14 per cent of its entire land area, causing a flood of environmental refugees. Tens of millions more people, mostly in poor countries, will be exposed to vector-borne diseases such as malaria, schistosomiasis and dengue fever.

As if this were not daunting enough, in 2002 the US National Academies of Science not only endorsed the IPCC's conclusions but produced a new report entitled *Abrupt Climate Change: inevitable surprises*, which argued that global warming may trigger 'large, abrupt and unwelcome regional or global climatic events' such as severe droughts and floods. The smooth curves of the climate models may hide the climate system's propensity to switch suddenly to new states, with barely imaginable results. Even the authors of the National Academies report were concerned that their discussion may curdle the blood of the public:

> It is important not to be fatalistic about the threats posed by abrupt climate change. Societies have faced both gradual and abrupt climate changes for millennia and have learned to adapt through various mechanisms, such as moving indoors, developing irrigation for crops, and migrating away from inhospitable regions.[8]

There is only one answer to the terrible problems that are expected to befall Earth if nothing is done: immediately begin reducing combustion of fossil fuels and keep reducing it until fossil fuels are largely phased out. In 1997, after ten years of hard-fought negotiations, the rich countries of the world agreed to the

Kyoto Protocol, which would see those countries reduce their emissions by around 5 per cent over ten to fifteen years. This would have been a significant first step, yet the agreement instantly came under attack from the fossil-fuel lobby in the United States, and the recalcitrant parties managed to insert so many loopholes in the protocol that, after several international meetings culminating in a conference in Marrakech in 2001, it would, if implemented, result in minimal reductions in the rich countries' greenhouse gas emissions. Despite this emasculation of the protocol, soon after his election in 2001 President Bush (whose victory was widely believed to have been financed by fossil-fuel giants such as Exxon and Enron) declared that even minimal emission cuts would be too costly and repudiated the protocol completely. Australia followed the US lead.

There has been one, and only one, reason for the reluctance of the rich countries of the world to reduce their emissions and so help to stave off environmental catastrophe—the perceived impact of reducing emissions on the rate of economic growth and especially the growth of a handful of powerful industries. This has been enough to jeopardise the future of the world. But on inspection the feared large economic costs of moving to a low-carbon economy prove illusory. Complicated economic models have been used to estimate the effects of cutting emissions on growth rates. These models systematically overestimate the negative effects on growth by making a series of assumptions that constrain how businesses can respond to the need to cut emissions. For example, they underestimate the opportunities for costless energy savings; they underestimate the rate of technological progress that would be stimulated by restrictions on the use of fossil fuels; and they wholly ignore the damage to the economy and human life that climate change itself will cause.

Yet, despite the fact that the models systematically overstate the costs of cutting emissions, they consistently produce estimates of reductions in growth rates that are, by any standard, minuscule. They typically conclude that cutting emissions as mandated in the Kyoto Protocol would see the GNP of the United States reduced by 1 per cent by 2012.[9] What does this figure mean? It means that with the required emission reductions GNP in 2012 is expected to be 1 per cent lower than it would otherwise have been. One per cent is a tiny amount. If nothing is done and the economy grows at 3 per cent a year over the period, GNP will be about 40 per cent higher by 2012. According to the models, if policies to reduce emissions as specified in the Kyoto Protocol were implemented, GNP would be 39 per cent higher by 2012. Put another way, instead of GNP reaching a level 40 per cent higher by, say, 1 June 2012, it will not reach that level until 1 October 2012. Yet in the face of these minute effects on economic growth, the United States has refused to play a part in reducing global greenhouse gas emissions. This is the growth fetish taken to an absurd degree. Confronted with a high probability of environmental catastrophe on Earth, the richest people on the planet—people who systematically overeat and who air-condition the outdoor forecourts of gas stations—are unwilling to wait an extra four months to increase their incomes by 40 per cent.[10] Understood this way, the growth fetish appears to be a form of madness.

The conquering spirit

The development mentality is the daily manifestation of growth fetishism. Every day governments and local authorities approve housing developments, shopping malls and roadway projects that despoil the remaining natural areas. The momentum of development seems to mesmerise decision makers. In a political environment where higher growth is regarded as a sacred duty of elected leaders, blocking a new shopping mall or a housing development is akin to taking a stance against progress itself, a challenge to one of history's immutable laws that few mayors or planning ministers are willing to embrace. As a result, cities around the world have expanded well beyond their optimum size, and new towns creep across the countryside, eating up remnants of the natural environment and diminishing the pleasantness of life for residents old and new.

Cities with millions of high-consumption residents act like huge vacuum cleaners, sucking in resources and then blowing out huge volumes of wastes that must be buried, dumped into the oceans, or vented into the atmosphere. Analysts have attempted to capture this process with the concept of the ecological footprint, which for each person is defined as 'the biologically productive areas necessary to continuously provide their resource supplies and absorb their wastes, using prevailing technology'. Each person in the United States requires 10.3 hectares of land to meet their consumption needs and absorb their waste products.[11] For the United Kingdom the figure is 5.2 hectares; for Japan, 4.3 hectares; for Germany, 5.3 hectares. This compares with an availability of land across the globe of 1.7 hectares per person, and 'footprints' of 1.2 hectares in China and 0.8 hectares in India. The cities of the West have been described as 'entropic black holes', a reference to the process by which materials and energy are transformed through use from a concentrated or organised form (for example, fossil fuels and phosphates to be used as fertilisers) into a dissipated and less useful form (carbon dioxide in the atmosphere and phosphoric chemicals in the waterways).

There must be something deeper to the growth imperative that explains why apparently rational people cannot accept that small sacrifices made now to protect the environment will produce long-term benefits for the economic system they so desperately want to preserve, quite apart from the wider goal of protecting ecological systems for their own sake. Indeed, protecting economic growth, and the system of private property on which it is based, has become one of our most powerful impulses, one that neoliberal political leaders trade on relentlessly. It is a religious urge. For the purest defenders of capitalism—the acolytes of Friedrich von Hayek and Milton Friedman, collected together in conservative parties and right-wing think tanks—environmentalists have displaced communists as the devil incarnate. Although they are not generally conscious of it, the radical Right are the intellectual keepers of the Old Testament canon according to which God created Nature for the benefit of man. Calls by environmentalists to respect the integrity of the natural world, and on this basis to stop certain commercial activities, are met with incomprehension and rage. The right to exploit the land is, after all, God-given. This toxic mix of divine endorsement and private property rights is most apparent in the ideology and political activity of the mining and agricultural industries.

Today almost the entire surface of Earth is managed by humans; very few wild and impenetrable areas remain. Wilderness must now be 'managed' in an attempt to prevent these last refuges from being overrun by human activity. But, of course, management itself is a method of human intervention. Expeditions now venture to Mount Everest to clean up the empty cans left by climbing parties. Dumps filled with domestic waste and leaking oil drums blight Antarctica. Park rangers in the wilderness of Southwest Tasmania complain of the litter left by tourists. Western environmentalism has produced many excellent utilitarian reasons for repairing the damage and being more responsible about the natural environment. But something deeper has been missed in the public debate—the psychological impact of the urge to conquer.

When the world was relatively empty—that is, for the first 2 million years of human history—people lived in communities that were islands of domestication in a sea of wilderness. Beyond the bounds of village or town, the world was full of mystery. The impact of the great explorers who mapped out new trading routes was as much psychological as economic, for they began to link all parts of the world and to destroy the idea that the world 'outside' was unknown. The maps could no longer be drawn with dragons at the edges of the seas. The work of the explorers was not just to turn Earth into a known entity, but to domesticate the globe and thus lay the foundations of a system that now links the fate of Colombian coffee farmers to the vagaries of European stock exchanges.

Restlessly searching for new places to conquer, the growth obsession has now turned its attention to outer space, and in the race to exploit space we find the very attitudes that have been the bane of environmentalism on Earth. Space is seen as an infinite exploitable resource and a limitless waste dump. Even more disquieting, it is seen by some as providing a refuge for humans should Earth become uninhabitable as a result of ecological catastrophe. If, unable to tame our appetite for more growth, we destroy the world we can move on to other worlds. In fact, we are now seeing the gamut of human exploitative activity played out in space, as if everything we have learnt on Earth has no bearing on our activities off it. For decades space agencies have been using the cosmos as a junkyard. Some debris is deliberately dumped there; redundant rocket stages, defunct satellites, wayward lens caps and dead batteries are simply abandoned. In 1990 the space shuttle recovered an old satellite and brought it back to Earth. Careful analysis by NASA scientists showed that it was speckled with urine and faecal matter that had been jettisoned by previous US and Russian space missions.

NASA now has a sophisticated monitoring program just to keep track of space debris. It can see around 400 000 pieces of space debris among more than a million smaller pieces, the detritus from dead satellites and discarded rocket stages—from large lumps of metal down to flecks of paint. Space agencies are now concerned because an object as small as 1 centimetre across travelling at an orbital velocity of 28 000 kilometres an hour has enough kinetic energy to knock out an average-sized spacecraft. US Air Force Space Command now catalogues and tracks 8000 larger fragments, so that it will not mistake the re-entry of a piece of orbital debris for an incoming ballistic missile and trigger a nuclear response.

The first answer of the authorities to the proliferation of space junk is not to stop making waste but to build barriers between the rubbish and us. The International Space Station—a multi-country venture due for completion in 2004—now incorporates a special space shield, known as the Whipple Bumper, which is expected to reduce the chances of a serious collision to one in ten. The space shuttle now flies backwards once it is in orbit because the engines at the rear are no longer needed once the shuttle is in space and can be used to absorb the impact of debris hitting the craft. Various schemes have been proposed for dealing with the problem of space junk, including construction of a garbage-collecting spacecraft, building lasers to vaporise debris, and pushing dying spacecraft further out into so-called grave-yard orbits.

In addition, as space-based activities expand, there is a growing danger to Earth's biosphere arising from activities aimed at sending objects into orbit. In one of the worst affected areas, spent booster stages from the Russian Tyrantum Space Centre crash back to Earth in Siberia. Many of the chemicals used in rockets are extremely dangerous to humans. For example, heptyl, one of the most toxic chemicals known and several times dead-lier than phosgene gas (a banned chemical weapon), is used in rocketry and is spread over large areas. More than 20 million hectares in Russia, and 81 million hectares in Kazakhstan, are believed to be polluted by chemical fallout from rockets launched from Russian cosmodromes. One of the results is the phenom-enon of 'yellow children'—children suffering from pathological jaundice, anaemia and disorders of the central nervous system. Although several kinds of US and European rockets use the same types of hazardous fuels as the Russian rockets, they are launched over the ocean in order to limit the effects on humans.

Of greater concern perhaps is the proliferation of nuclear material in orbit around Earth. In August 1998 NASA executed a fly-by manoeuvre by the *Cassini* space probe, which carries 33 kilograms of plutonium. *Cassini* approached Earth at a speed of more than 133 000 kilometres an hour and passed a little more than 1000 kilometres above the southern Pacific Ocean. According to NASA's own environmental impact statement, a collision with Earth's atmosphere would have seen *Cassini* release 400 000 curies of plutonium as fine particles, which would in one fell swoop more than double the amount of human-made plutonium in the atmosphere. The global health effects would have been severe.

Commercial opportunity is the handmaiden of the conquering spirit latterly expressed in the invasion of space. Private sector investment in space-related activities is expanding enormously and is already giving rise to intense pressure for unfettered access to space for commercial purposes. At present most interest is centred on the use of orbital space for communications since satellites now play a crucial role in television, telecommunications, remote sensing, and global positioning systems. There is little doubt that in a decade or two space tourism will became a must for the trendy rich, bored with private tropical islands and Antarctic flights. People are already booking seats to the Moon.

The commercial opportunities provided by the exploitation of space are changing attitudes to it. Segments of the space-development lobby believe that early UN treaties governing space should be jettisoned so that private property in extraterrestrial resources can be established through homestead rights, or squatting. They argue that whoever gets there first and establishes a base should be able to claim ownership of the territory. According to some activists, the United States should simply pass a law directing its courts to recognise any extraterrestrial land claim by any private entity that has established a settlement. One space entrepreneur, Jim Benson, believes it should be easier still: rather than having to establish a human settlement, if someone can put a robot on a celestial body such as an asteroid and bring back mineral resources, they should be able to claim title to it. Benson is planning to do just that and has declared: 'If the UN doesn't like it, they can send a tank up to my asteroid . . .'.[12]

Human settlement of space is high on the agenda of some groups. The National Space Society—a surprisingly influential organisation dedicated to furthering the exploration and development of space—is committed to the colonisation of space by humans. It has declared that, when human settlement was first proposed, 'the idea that people could have an interesting life in a space station was seen as unlikely. "Who", we were asked, "would want to live in such a controlled environment?"' Without any apparent irony, it answered its own question: 'Nowadays, of course, the proliferation of integrated shopping/entertainment/residential malls answers that question: lots of people do'.

Through this exploration and commercial activity humanity's attitudes towards and relationship with outer space are being transformed, and the transformation is along predictable lines. Instead of being a place of mystery and awe, space is becoming, like Earth, a repository of new resources that can serve the voracious growth machine. Instead of the age-old respect deriving from its inherent distance and vastness, space must earn 'respect' by providing obstacles to its own exploitation. Thus near-Earth orbits will in all probability be cleaned up because the proliferation of orbital junk threatens the profitability of space-based economic activities. We lack an ethics of space,[13] and the exploitation of outer space reflects the dominant philosophy of value, one that environmentalism has challenged at its very core.

A philosophical transition

Although its more obtuse adherents are prone to deny it, neoliberalism is based on a particular philosophy of value. Instrumental value theory maintains that, while humans are valuable in and of themselves, the non-human world is valuable only insofar as it contributes to the wellbeing of humans. Thus the natural world has only instrumental value. Neoliberalism is therefore properly described as an anthropocentric, or human-centred, philosophy. A number of arguments have been advanced to sustain the belief that humans have intrinsic value—their rationality, their ability to communicate symbolically, the possession of a soul, and the belief that they are 'God's chosen creatures'.[14] But the intrinsic value of humans is not at issue. The philosophical question that has been posed by environmentalists relates to the value of the natural world, and the deep political influence of the modern environment movement arises from the fact that the answer it gives resonates strongly with sections of the public.

Three types of instrumentalist attitude to Nature can be identified in neoliberal writings. The first is the belief that the environment is valuable to humans because physical resources provide economic value, so that the value of Nature is measured by its value in the market. Since multiplying the volume of goods in the marketplace improves human life, and human life has intrinsic value, unrestrained economic expansion and exploitation of the environment are justified. Clearly, this belief radically separates humans from the natural world and subordinates the latter to the former, both philosophically and in practice. Separation of the two carries the attribution of various qualities to each, qualities that often form pairs of opposites. Ecofeminists have pointed out the dualistic character of the radical separation of the human world and the natural world—the implicit distinctions between culture and Nature, reason and emotion, male and female. In these dualisms Nature is seen as female, subordinate, chaotic and tribal, while 'culture' is seen as masculine, superior, rational and ordered. This view of 'man and Nature' is, therefore, not just anthropocentric but androcentric, or male-centred.

The second instrumentalist view of Nature remains preoccupied with the physical transformation of resources but recognises the physical limits to material growth. The lessons of ecology have been learnt, at least at a superficial level. Although this view is less inclined to favour unfettered exploitation, it takes a longer term perspective, acknowledging the importance of intergenerational equity and the idea of maximum sustainable yield. Like the crude instrumentalist view, it remains thoroughly anthropocentric and based on self-interest, but it is enlightened self-interest. It forms the philosophical basis for 'environmental economics', an extension of neoliberalism to accommodate resource limits. The books by David Pearce, such as *Blueprint for a Green Economy*,[15] are typical of this world view, and the fact that the ideas could be so readily adopted by Margaret Thatcher suggests that it poses no challenge to growth fetishism but seeks only to rescue growth from its self-destructive impulses.

The third instrumentalist view, softer still, argues that instrumental value can be had from preserving rather than exploiting some aspects of the natural environment. For example, preserving tropical forests rather than allowing them to be logged may provide more value to humans compared with the market value of the lumber. Environmental philosopher Warwick Fox suggests that there are four principal arguments for the preservationist view: preservation of genetic resources for future use, for scientific study, for recreation, and for aesthetic inspiration.[16] These 'values' of the environment have been annexed by environmental economists and described as new types of economic value with names such as 'existence value', 'option value' and 'bequest value'. New techniques have been developed to put a price on these attributes of the natural world, including surveys to determine potential consumers' 'willingness to pay' to protect rather than exploit (the so-called contingent valuation method). As in conventional economics texts, this way of thinking begins by imagining the natural environment as a set of commodities with alternative uses, uses that may have more or less instrumental value arising from protection or exploitation, depending on how the numbers turn out.

Environmentalism begins from an intuitive rejection of all instrumentalist approaches. It accepts that the natural world has *intrinsic* value rather than instrumental value. In other words, the value of the environment is not dependent on humans attaching value to it, and certainly not on humans deciding whether it contributes to their economic welfare. A number of reasons have been advanced in favour of the intrinsic value of nature, including the idea that organisms strive for life or to reproduce, which are ends in themselves, and the ethic of animal liberation, in which all sentient beings qualify for moral considerability.[17] One of the most influential arguments is the 'land ethic' of Aldo Leopold, summarised in the following statement: 'A thing is right when it tends to preserve the integrity, stability and beauty of a biotic community. It is wrong when it tends otherwise'.[18]

In contrast, the stance of 'transpersonal ecology' is centred on the notion that only the ego-involved, contracted self can imagine itself to be distinct from the natural world and that expansion of the self beyond the boundaries of the personal necessarily means that one's awareness, and ground of concern, extends to the natural world. Mere moralising is not enough and can in fact be alienating to the public; the real task is to build not so much an environmental ethic but an ecological consciousness.[19] Transpersonal ecology is a philosophical reassertion of 'participating consciousness' and therefore goes beyond mere rational appreciation of our relationship with the natural world. It holds promise of a transformation of personal identity as well as understanding because it poses the question: With what do I identify? Put as starkly as possible: Do I identify with the natural world in which I find myself or with a pair of Diesel jeans? Do I work for Saatchi and Saatchi or Greenpeace? These questions are being confronted by growing numbers of young citizens in post-scarcity societies.

It is precisely at this point that we comprehend the moral function of growth fetishism and its personal counterpart, consumerism. For the preoccupation with growth and material acquisition inevitably causes consciousness to shrink. The mind that 'meditates' at the shopping mall can never expand to encompass the intrinsic values of the natural world; it can only look upon it as a mine that provides the resources to make the goods that are consumed or as a dump into which can be discarded the goods we have tired of. The rationality of the market constantly impels us to see the world in this way. Despite its claims to universalism, the rationality of the market is in no sense timeless and universal. As the early sociologist Max Weber argued, the essence of modern capitalism lies in its peculiar form of rationality.[20] Market exchange and wage labour are the pillars of capitalism; market exchange is fundamentally rational in the sense that all commitments other than pure economic self-interest are irrelevant. Moreover, all moral claims, family and clan loyalties, rites, obligations and social traditions are stripped away. In previous eras, the act of exchange was filled with social as well as economic significance, and the economics of traditional societies lay largely in systems of gift exchange. As Rogers Brubaker has written, 'The market is the paradigm of rationality in this double sense, for market exchange, more than any other type of activity, is determined by the deliberate and calculating pursuit of self-interest and is free from the multifarious fetters of tradition and the capricious influence of feelings'.[21]

In other words, the marketplace is intensely impersonal, a place where actions are motivated by self-interested calculation between distinct individuals. It allows the full expression of instrumentalist desire. Advanced forms of monetary measurement and monetary exchange permit the depersonalisation of market transactions and the dominance of instrumental calculation. Not only is the natural world transformed into a set of more or less valuable resources, but other humans are objectified as rational calculating machines devoid of social value. Rather than weighing up a range of consequences from an exchange—financial implications, social obligations, considerations of caste and class—free individuals in the market can measure the consequences of their actions by one parameter alone, the monetary balance to be had from the exchange. Weber wrote, 'From a purely technical point of view, money is the most "perfect" means of economic calculation. That is, it is formally the most rational means of orienting economic activity. Calculation in terms of money is thus the specific means of rational economic provision'.[22]

The material progress of the industrial revolution was thus built on the idea of calculability. Weber stressed the importance of calculability as the basis for efficient capital accounting and thus profit making. Rational decision making depends wholly on the ability to evaluate outcomes. There can be no place for intuition, let alone the expanded awareness of transpersonal ecology and environmentalism. The rationality of our economic world, therefore, is peculiar to the economic system that emerged with the industrial revolution. The dominance of instrumental rationality has seen a psychological shift of historic importance, one with no precedent in the history of humankind. This is not to decry the value of rationality as such; rather, it is to recognise rationality's specific form in Western society and, above all, to point to its crippling effects when it is allowed to dominate all else.

Of course, this is precisely the error of modern economics, sometimes characterised as 'autistic'. The sharp distinction between the observer and the observed is expressed in economics by the archetypal situation in which the economic agent, known as 'rational economic man', confronts the material world of commodities. The agent acts on the physical world, which now consists of 'resources', in order to satisfy human desires. In no sense does rational economic man participate in the world. In contrast with other modes of self-awareness in which the world is fraught with meaning, the world is essentially dead.

In the end, it is possible that as a result of prodigious efforts and great technological leaps resource use and waste emissions will be reduced to very low levels. That might defer the physical problems of sustainability, perhaps for a long time; but the real environmental issue is what our misuse of the natural world does to the psychology of humans rather than the economy. The task is to bring the natural world 'back to life' and for this we need to go beyond philosophies rooted in the market.

Environmentalism and social democracy

The growth fetish is sustained by one or other of the first two instrumentalist views described in the previous section—

unrestrained exploitation of the environment or the more enlightened approach in which self-interest is preserved by taking a longer term perspective. The only difference is that one view looks to short-term GDP growth while the other considers what is needed to maximise the growth rate over time. The third instrumentalist view accepts that improvements in human welfare can be had if some economic growth is traded for preservation of some environmental benefits that would otherwise be destroyed. It is the basis for alternative measures to GDP that attempt to capture some of the non-market costs and benefits of the environment, notably the Genuine Progress Indicator discussed in Chapter 2. Yet this view remains a prisoner of the commodity view of the world, only now the natural world is considered to supply an additional set of commodities for human consumption. In the parlance of neoclassical economics, the utility function is augmented by non-consumptive values. It happens that many of the 'goods' in question are not produced and sold in the marketplace, although there is no shortage of proposals to privatise lands, rivers and seas so that commodities such as recreation and genetic stocks can be brought into the economic calculus.

The third of the instrumentalist philosophies is as far as even the most progressive thinkers of the Third Way go. Steeped in the philosophical legacy of social democracy, they find no comfortable place in their intellectual framework or everyday thoughts for the natural environment. In his seminal book *The Third Way*, Anthony Giddens makes a series of observations on 'ecology' and social democracy, but he struggles with the terminology of environmentalism, committing one solecism after another. At no point does he seem to recognise that environmentalism represents a fundamental challenge to the philosophical infrastructure of both social democracy and neoliberalism. It is as if in writing *The Third Way* he decided that a chapter on the environment was needed because, after all, along with the women's movement, it is the most important social movement of the last half of the 20th century. Deferentially, he set about to fill some pages, but it turns out to be one section of one chapter that quickly segues into an extraneous discussion of 'risk' that ends with social democracy and 'ecology' as far apart as ever.

The question of the political alignment of social democracy and environmentalism remains unanswered by thinkers and politicians of the Third Way. Because policies to protect the environment sometimes involve structural adjustment that means job losses for low-income workers, opponents of environmentalism have often characterised the movement as a middle-class indulgence. This has led to an uneasy coexistence of the environment movement and the welfare sector for two decades or more. While both are placed on the 'progressive' side of politics, welfare groups tend to see environmentalists as preoccupied with fashionable concerns at the expense of the real concerns of the poor, while environmentalists are often frustrated that welfare groups define wellbeing too narrowly and cannot see that environmental degradation affects the poor more than the rich. These differing views have spilled over into public disagreements about petrol taxes and carbon taxes in particular, with welfare groups accusing environmentalists of failing to recognise that higher fuel prices unduly disadvantage the poor.

The effects of a carbon tax—a tax on the carbon content of fossil fuels—are complicated and the equity implications are not at all straightforward. The effects will tend to fall more heavily on poorer households, but they are in general not as large as imagined. In the United States, the poorest 10 per cent of households (who receive substantial transfer payments and non-monetary benefits) spend less than 4 per cent of total outlays on petrol, while middle-income households commit 4–6 per cent of total spending.[23] Although the industries that are negatively affected by a carbon tax tend to have a greater preponderance of blue-collar workers, effective use of the tax revenue—in reducing taxes on payrolls or employers' pension payments, for example—can produce a net benefit for employment.

As a general rule, inequality is affected much more by decisions about how to use the revenue from a new tax than by the tax itself. Proposals that would see higher taxes on environmentally damaging activities, with the revenue used to reduce taxes on employment and investment, are known under the rubric of ecological tax reform. Europe has taken this idea further than other OECD countries, and there is little doubt that it will be a key plank of tax policy in the future. The general lesson of work in this area is that a properly developed set of policies can induce in an economy structural change that both is beneficial for the environment and leads to an improvement in social equity. The 'double dividend' of reduced emissions and increased employment is simultaneously a contribution to sustainability and equity, so that much of the disagreement between environmentalists and welfare groups can be resolved.

But the equity implications of environment protection go much further. In public debate the emphasis has been on the immediate distributional impacts of measures to preserve the environment: the distributional aspects of failing to prevent degradation of the environment have been almost wholly ignored. The simple fact is that in almost every case the poor suffer far more than the rich from degradation of the natural environment, an observation that applies to both today's poor and the poor of the future. In the important case of air pollution, in general wealthier people can more easily afford to live in areas with low pollution while poorer people tend to live closer to busy roads and industrial estates.[24] On the face of it, we would expect high levels of atmospheric lead to have a greater impact on poorer people than on wealthier people. An Australian study of lead levels in children showed that children from families with annual incomes below $20 000 had substantially higher lead levels than children from families with incomes above $20 000.[25] Thus, the failure to discourage lead use will mean that the IQs of children from poorer families will be reduced by more than the IQs of children from wealthier families. The World Bank reports that children in Bangkok lose an average of four or more IQ points by the age of seven because of exposure to high levels of lead in the air.[26]

The international equity implications are particularly acute in the case of climate change, since people in developing countries are expected to suffer more severe impacts. They are also in a weaker position to defend themselves against changes in the climate, including the effects of more frequent and intense heat waves, floods and droughts and rising sea levels. Poorer households are more likely to live in flood-prone areas and will bear a disproportionately high burden of the increased flood damage arising from climate change. It is perverse for social welfare groups in rich countries to object to rises in fuel prices when the most impoverished people in developing countries will suffer severely from rich countries' failure to reduce their greenhouse gas emissions. Moreover, in the rich countries themselves the children and grandchildren of the poor will be least able to escape the effects of climate change.

Neoclassical economists and conservative commentators have traditionally characterised environmental preservation as a 'luxury good'—that is, a good for which demand increases with increasing income. In the case of nations, it has been suggested that as poor countries industrialise environmental quality will initially deteriorate but as they become richer they will express a greater 'preference' for environmental quality and things will improve. This relationship is known as the 'environmental Kuznets curve'. Of course, environmental standards are political decisions. There is nothing ineluctable about the quality of the environment, and it is perfectly feasible for two nations on the same growth trajectory to have radically different standards. In the case of forest preservation, such a view suggests that wealthier people derive more benefit from preserving forests than poorer people. For most people, however, preserving forests is an ethical rather than an economic concern; they consider it strange to characterise the forests as a 'good' to be traded off among others, like so many sausages. Nevertheless, the question is an important social and political one. Are the rich more concerned about preserving the forests than the poor? If they are, they might be thought to enjoy greater non-utilitarian benefits than the poor. This is an empirical matter, but survey evidence indicates that there is no significant difference between more and less wealthy households in attitudes to preservation.[27]

If our focus shifts from class differences to the condition in which people find themselves under consumer capitalism, environmentalism has a great deal to tell us about modern alienation. Marx, preoccupied with the transition from an agricultural economy to capitalist industry dominated by wage labour, located alienation in the separation of workers from their products. It is argued here that alienation in consumer capitalism is intimately associated with how we relate to consumption in a society dominated by acquisitiveness and the ideology of marketing. We have also seen that the instrumentalist philosophy that characterises production under capitalism follows from the radical separation of humans from the natural world and the treatment of Nature as a catalogue of resources that exist to be exploited. Whether resources are finite or not is irrelevant from this point of view: an infinity of resources would serve only to extend the period over which we delude ourselves with the belief that the path to contentment lies in the accumulation of goods. This is perhaps the core difference between environmental economics and the nascent discipline known as ecological economics. Environmental economics is an unapologetic extension of the old economics, incorporating some new elements in the individual consumer's set of preferences. In this there is nothing new. In contrast, the approach of ecological economics abandons the imperialism of the old economics and begins from an understanding of ecological processes and the essential role of humans in them. Whether based on ecological science or philosophical intuition, ecological economics affirms humans' unity with the natural world, rather than their separation from it. Closely associated with the idea of a stationary state (a subject discussed in the next chapter), the new discipline is helping to lay the intellectual and philosophical foundations for a post-growth society.

The post-growth society

Political downshifting

The transition to a post-growth society will be just as far-reaching as the transition from feudalism to industrial capitalism or from industrial capitalism to global consumer capitalism. It will fundamentally transform power relationships, social institutions, our relationships with others, our ethical rules, our attitudes to the natural environment and, ultimately, our consciousness.

Radical in its implications as it might be, the case for a transition to a post-growth society is by no means far-fetched or utopian. Many people in rich countries have already made a decision to reduce their work, incomes and consumption. Juliet Schor provides an assessment of the 'downshifting' phenomenon in the United States: 'Downshifters are opting out of excessive consumerism, choosing to have more leisure and balance in their schedules, a slower pace of life, more time with their kids, more meaningful work, and daily lives that line up squarely with their deepest values'.[1] Her evidence suggests that among the downshifters are people from a broad range of social classes and income groups; they are not merely stressed-out yuppies.

Downshifting frequently requires major changes to lifestyles and personal priorities, but it does not mean plunging oneself into poverty. Few downshifters are driven by ideology or religion; most are ordinary people who have decided it is in their interests to step off the materialist treadmill and take up a more balanced and rewarding life. Schor reports the results of a US survey in which a remarkable 19 per cent of the adult population declared that in the previous five years they had voluntarily decided to make a change in their lives that resulted in making less money. This fifth of the American population excluded those taking a scheduled retirement but included those voluntarily switching to lower paid jobs, choosing to reduce their hours of work, and deciding to stay at home and look after their children.

A similar survey in Australia found that 23 per cent of 30–60 year olds had downshifted, citing as their reasons a desire for more balance and control in their lives, more time with their families and more personal fulfilment.[2] The downshifters, often people with no more than average incomes, expressed a desire to do something more meaningful with their lives, and to achieve this aim they considered it was necessary to consume less, work less and slow down. In the US survey, before their life change more than half of the downshifters worked over 40 hours a week (with 28 per cent working over 50 hours); afterwards nearly half worked fewer than 30 hours (and only 7 per cent worked more than 50 hours).[3] In the Australian study, around 30 per cent of downshifters reduced their working hours while around 23 per cent took a lower-paying job, 20 per cent changed careers and 20 per cent stopped work altogether.[4]

For every downshifter who has made the change there are others who wish for the same. The *Yearning for Balance* report discussed in Chapter 1 identifies a fundamental disconnection between what people see as important for their own, their family's and their nation's wellbeing and how they and their fellow citizens actually lead their lives. They want their lives to be grounded in the basic values of family closeness, friendship, and individual and social responsibility, but they see their society and their own lives mired in consumerism, selfishness and exploitation of the natural world. Downshifters are motivated above all by the desire to bring the daily reality of their lives into harmony with their deeply held values. To make the transition, they take a crucial but simple psychological leap: they decide that they will no longer judge their own worth by the amount they earn and consume.

While the downshifters might be seen as standard bearers in the revolt against consumerism, the social revolution required to make the transition to a post-growth society will not come about solely through the personal decisions of determined individuals. The forces devoted to buttressing the ideology of growth fetishism and obsessive consumption are difficult to resist, and they are boosted immeasurably by governments' obsession with growth at all costs. Making the transition to the new dispensation demands a politics of downshifting. Political downshifting can be defined as the entrenchment within popular culture, public and private institutions and, ultimately, government of a predisposition to promote the quality of social and individual life rather than surrendering to the demands of the market.

The politics of downshifting find a natural home in the new politics of contemporary social movements. Bypassing the politics of the entrenched parties, now characterised by instinctive conservatism, personal opportunism, executive control and the power of lobbyists to overturn repeatedly popular preference, the new politics is the politics of direct participation pioneered by the environment movement and inherited by the 'anti-globalisation' protest movement and the *No Logo* generation. Indeed, the vision of a post-growth society may become the focus of social change around which the modern protest movements coalesce and recapture the democratic electoral process. The two-party system of parliamentary elections suited post-war social democracy well, but the era of neoliberalism has left only the illusion of choice between two parties both in the grip of the growth fetish. The roots of the established political parties are sunk too deeply in the old politics and new parties must emerge. The capitulation of social democratic and labour parties to neoliberalism has left them soulless and they are now staffed, for the most part, by people who have cashed in their youthful enthusiasm for the perquisites of office and traded their policies of radical social change for a media strategy. If these parties were to play a role in bringing about the post-growth society they would need to extricate themselves from their Faustian bargain and undergo a process of wholesale renewal.

Eudemonism: the politics of happiness

The belief that more money makes us happier has all the characteristics of an addiction, one on which the survival of consumer capitalism depends. But a politics that has the courage to penetrate beneath the surface of material desire, and to promise rich lives instead of lives of riches, has an intuitive appeal for all but the most hard-bitten victims of consumer consciousness.

The social basis of discontent in modern society is not so much lack of income; it is loneliness, boredom, depression, alienation, self-doubt and the ill-health that goes with them. 'Social exclusion' is not so much exclusion from the structures of production and consumption; it is exclusion from social relationships and modes of self-understanding that confer acknowledgment, self-worth and meaning. Most of the problems of modern society are not the result of inadequate incomes; they are the result of social structures, ideologies and cultural forms that prevent people from realising their potential and leading satisfying lives in their communities. A post-growth society will consciously promote the social structures and activities that actually improve individual and community wellbeing. It will aim to provide a social environment in which people can pursue true individuality, rather than the pseudo-individuality that is now obtained through spending on brand names and manufactured lifestyles.

The post-growth society will diverge sharply from what is now considered natural or unchangeable and will therefore be met with resistance. Opposition will come from those who stand to lose political influence and economic power and from the ideologists of growth in politics, the media and the universities. Above all, the notion will challenge many ordinary people, who will struggle against accepting what they know to be true—that becoming richer will not bring them more worthwhile lives.

For the great majority of people in rich countries the human condition is no longer dominated by an ever-present need to provide for survival and to accumulate assets to guard against lean times. The defining struggle is no longer between proletarians and capitalists about how to divide the surplus of the production process; today it is about how to live a genuine life in a social structure that manufactures 'individuality' and celebrates superficiality. Once the economic problem had been solved, before history had allowed time for people to decide what to do next, the marketers filled the vacuum of consciousness with their message of consumption. Although most people intuitively understand that their condition is determined above all by a need to find fulfilment in a social environment that puts income before purpose, they act as if there is nothing wrong because they know not what else to do. The vision of a post-growth society answers the question of what to do next.

I have characterised the conjunction of Western society's preoccupation with economic growth and the manifest failure of higher incomes to improve wellbeing as the great contradiction of modern capitalism. Refusal to recognise the contradiction is the reason for the decline of the political Left. By implicitly conceding that more growth is the measure of success, the Left found it increasingly difficult to argue that various forms of socialism could outperform 'turbo-capitalism' on its own territory. This is why the politics of the Third Way feel false: despite its claims to inclusiveness and community building, these things have been made contingent on the need to promote economic growth. A genuine critique of consumer capitalism, and the plethora of troubles associated with it, must be based firstly on a rejection of the growth fetish.

When people on the Left consider possible alternatives to neoliberalism, they are conditioned to think in terms of rival structures of ownership and the organisation of production. Thus classical socialists advocated workers' cooperatives or communes, 20th century communists created state enterprises along with soviets and collective farms, and social democrats have defined their philosophy as a judicious mix of public and private ownership. Supporters of capitalism, and especially its purified neoliberal form, identify private ownership of the means of production as the defining feature of the system. The terminology speaks for itself. Capitalism is so called because the motivating force of production and social organisation is ownership of private capital; socialism is so called because it is centred on social ownership of the means of production. Political philosophies whose competing claims have defined the history of the world for the last two centuries have been at one in identifying the central social problem—how to produce and distribute material wealth. But now that in rich countries the economic problem has been solved, the axis of political debate and social change must move away from the production sphere and the forms of ownership of the means of production.

Within social democratic and labour parties there have been bitter disputes between 'reformers' who want to discard clauses in party platforms that call for the 'socialisation of the means of production, distribution and exchange' and those on the traditional Left who have defended the principle. The traditional Left continues to defend the socialisation objective, long after it has given up hope of implementing it, because it is dismayed at the capitulation of the reformers to the markets; in turn, the reformers have been bent on transforming social democracy into a form of soft-edged neoliberalism. Thus for the traditional Left the socialisation objective remains a symbol only, a symbol of a desire for something radically different from unfettered capitalism but with no clear idea of what this might be. This is not to say that the question of public versus private ownership no longer has political importance: social justice and citizenship require public ownership of certain industries and activities. But the ownership question is no longer the vital one in post-scarcity societies, and for this reason a post-growth political philosophy does not represent any fundamental threat to private property.

Eudemonia was used by Aristotle to capture the idea of happiness or wellbeing arising from the full realisation of human potential, and I have adopted the rather awkward term 'eudemonism' as a short-hand expression for what I am advocating in this book.[5] In my usage, eudemonism concerns not just a system of ethics but also a political ideology that argues for an organisation of society that promotes the full realisation of human potential through, in the first instance, proper appreciation of the sources of wellbeing. While the program set forth here would, if taken up, represent a profound challenge to capitalism as we know it, it cannot be characterised as socialist. It reaffirms a necessary role for public ownership, but it does not propose any expropriation of private property. It is, however, anti-capitalist in the sense that it argues that society and governments should no longer cede special significance to the objectives or moral claims of the owners of capital. For the most part, capitalism itself has answered the demands that inspired 19th century socialism—the demands for an end to exploitation at work, for an end to widespread poverty, for social justice, and for representative democracy. But attainment of these goals has only brought deeper sources of social unease—manipulation by marketers, obsessive materialism, environmental degradation, endemic alienation, and loneliness. In short, just as women sacrificed liberation in the pursuit of equality, in the marketing society, we seek fulfilment but settle for abundance. Prisoners of plenty, we have the freedom to consume instead of the freedom to find our place in the world.

The post-growth society envisaged here does share something fundamental with socialism. As Andre Gorz has observed, 'Socialism may . . . be understood as the positive response to the disintegration of social bonds ensuing from the commodity and competitive relations characteristic of capitalism'.[6] Eudemonism too is motivated by an understanding of the corrosive effects of capitalism on social bonds, but it differs in two respects. First, it attributes this erosion of social bonds not so much to the depredations of the capital–worker relationship but to the social disintegration associated with excessive consumption in the marketing society. Second, the problem of capitalism is not only the disintegration of social bonds but also the loss of self that characterises the marketing society. We need to recover the security and integration of pre-modern societies, societies

> in which the unity of work and life, of society and community, of the individual and the collective, of culture

and politics, of economy and morality, is re-established; in which the functional requirements of the system coincide with the aims of everyone, and the meaning of each person's life coincides with the meaning of History.[7]

The price of abundance has been the disintegration of community and the disintegration of self. Reintegration can now occur at a higher level, in conditions that permit the flowering of individual and collective potential unconstrained by material want, political oppression and primitive beliefs. The 'aims of everyone' have not changed in essence over the centuries, but they have been pursued in increasingly false and futile ways. Eudemonism, then, is a political and social system whose functional requirements are consistent with the need for people to find fulfilment in their lives.

Such a society will engender and reflect a historic transformation of consciousness, one consistent with the process of individualisation. In contrast with the historical trend, in which economic considerations have invaded and come to dominate more and more aspects of life and social organisation, eudemonism will see the displacement of economic rationality by other forms of rationality, so that the former is confined to a smaller and smaller domain—indeed, to the domain where it properly belongs. Eudemonism will see the flourishing of the rationality of community over that of self-interest and the spread of the ecological rationality of intrinsic value in place of the instrumental exploitation of the natural world. True sustainability will become possible in a society that has gone beyond economic growth and ever-increasing consumption. Not only will the pressure of consumption be diminished, but governments will be less inclined to abandon policies that are essential to sustainability because of pressure from business. The principal claim of business—that it is essential to improving the growth rate—will evaporate. In no sense does this mean that we must revert to 'primitive lifestyles'. There is no reason why we could not continue to benefit from the enormous creativity of humanity. But we could use that creativity to tread more lightly on Earth, to develop new ways of protecting the environment, and to live richer lives in our communities at the same time.

As the emphasis on consumption and paid work is wound back, new space will be opened up for cultural, educational and community work and for participation in meaningful leisure. Not only would more time be available for these activities; their value will also be increased once the leviathan of the market is reduced to its proper size. This will augur a deeper transformation, a move away from activities carried out for instrumental reasons—the production of goods and services destined for the market—towards activities that are valuable in themselves. We will benefit from these activities as much from the doing of them as from the outputs generated. In this way, much more of people's daily activity will be fulfilling in itself and provide the opportunity for growth of character. This type of activity, which is currently classed as unproductive, will be understood to be productive because it produces the self and reproduces community, and the value of these activities will be apparent from their manifest contribution to the wellbeing of all.

In the new dispensation, the function of government will be reoriented so that it provides sustenance to life-affirming activities outside the market. Indeed, the function of the state will change radically—from one devoted principally to providing the conditions demanded by the economy (and especially global financial markets) and correcting 'market failures', to one devoted to protecting and enhancing the 'life-communities' that are the true source of human wellbeing. One of the central functions of the state will be to redistribute income generated in the money economy to the household economy, in order to sustain the activities carried out in this realm, including parenting and caring for the sick and elderly.[8] Among the transforming consequences of the rebalancing of time will be to even up the emphasis attached to unpaid as opposed to paid work. For, although women have increasingly achieved equality in the arena of paid work, the fact that unpaid work in the household remains predominantly the domain of women has kept it in the dismissive shadow of the economy. Greater equality in the domestic sphere remains a desirable goal, and greater value attached to household and community work will facilitate the process. As long as political structures cede pre-eminence to the economy, those activities that lie outside the economy are less attractive and less socially valuable. When the household sphere resumes its proper place and is given its due, men will be more attracted to it and both women and men will feel validated by their dedication to it. In general, the world of the market economy is dominated by masculine values and male consciousness—competitiveness, hierarchy, instrumental rationality, the accumulation of status through display, and appropriation of the external world. The household is dominated by female values and forms of consciousness—intuitive appreciation, collaborative structures, empathy and caring.

A rebalancing of these worlds will allow for a realignment of these values and forms of consciousness and permit the healthy expression of male and female values in both women and men.

One of the many benefits of this eudemonistic program is that it will encourage a reinvigoration of democracy. People are demoralised and marginalised from the political process. Daily they are told that the economy is too complex and important to be ruled by the ignorant masses and that decisions must be left to experts who understand the intricacies of the system. There is, however, deep disquiet about leaving it to the experts, not least because the experts have been promising bliss for a long time, generating a growing and disturbing cynicism. Yet, as long as the economy remains paramount, there is no alternative but to leave it to the experts. When the economy is cut down to size—the size justified by its contribution to wellbeing—people will feel their voice counts once again and they will be freed to participate in democratic processes at every level, including the international level. In these circumstances, we can expect a flowering of civic culture, in which political ideas—for decades suppressed by the market's intolerance of the unorthodox—can once again be debated around the dinner tables and in the bars of every town.

Starting the transition

It might be thought that the post-growth society is an appealing utopia that could never be achieved in practice. This doubt can be answered by pointing to practical measures that, when implemented, will initiate the transition from today's consumer capitalism to a post-growth social formation. Here is not the place to go into detail, but a number of demands stand out as the basis for a politics of downshifting.

Work

Reduction in working hours is the core demand for the transition to a post-growth society. Overwork not only propels overconsumption but is the cause of severe social dysfunction, with ramifications for physical and psychological health as well as family and community life. The natural solution to this is the redistribution of work, a process that could benefit both the unemployed and the overworked. Moves to limit overwork, as with France's legislation for a 35-hour week, directly confront the obsession with growth at all costs. Despite initial complaints from employers the sky has not fallen in over Gaul and there is already evidence of a cultural change in which workers are finding that they are being liberated from the compulsion to earn more than they need.

In his 1930 essay on life after growth, John Maynard Keynes suggested a 15-hour week would suffice as a reasonable long-term goal for paid work. After all, at a typical rate of growth in labour productivity of 2 per cent, if the extra fruits of labour were taken in reduced working time rather than higher incomes, we could reduce working hours from 40 to 15 hours a week within 50 years while maintaining current income levels. A 30-hour week could be achieved in ten to fifteen years with unchanged levels of income.

The move to shorter working time would be much more than a workplace policy: it would form the centrepiece of far-reaching social change. In the first place, people would be freed to spend more time with their families, in their communities, and pursuing the activities that they find personally fulfilling. Second, the declining emphasis on paid work would be accompanied by a waning preoccupation with consumption activities and together these would constitute an assault on the role of consumption in constructing identity. Some of the time freed from the compulsion to work and consume could be devoted to education and self-betterment.

Marketing

The growth fetish is sustained by an unrelenting barrage of marketing and advertising—messages that have invaded and occupied public space and private lives. They fill our homes, our leisure activities and our workplaces. The transition to a post-growth society would begin by imposing restrictions on the quantity and nature of marketing messages, by first banning advertising and sponsorship from all public spaces and restricting advertising time on television and radio. Tax laws could be changed so that the costs of advertising are no longer a deductible business expense but come out of profits. Second, we should demand legislation requiring truth in advertising, a move that would require nothing more than enshrining in legislation and enforcing the industry's own code of conduct under which advertisers are banned from making misleading claims or ascribing to products properties that they do not possess. Third, in order to provide a daily respite from the torrent of commercial messages and allow people to cultivate their relationships, especially with children, television broadcasts hours should be restricted.

Measuring progress

The use of GDP as the measure of national progress conditions the way we think about social change and skews social policy in favour of growth fetishism. A Charter of National Accounting Honesty would require statistical agencies to develop and disseminate accurate indicators of national progress. The national accounts could carry a prominent warning: 'Under no circumstances should these figures be interpreted as measures of national progress or social improvement'.

International

Taxation and regulatory measures should be used to limit opportunities for new investment in rich countries and encourage suitable investment in developing countries where economic growth can improve wellbeing. Short-term speculative capital movements should be severely penalised by an international transactions tax. The three major institutions of global economic management—the World Trade Organization, the International Monetary Fund and the World Bank—should be made democratic and accountable with national representatives nominated by an elected panel of citizens. These organisations should be required to pursue their original goals of promoting development in the poorest nations and justice and sustainability everywhere.

When growth is no longer fetishised, foreign relations will be determined much less by the demands of arms traders, big pharmaceutical companies and investment houses, and a truly ethical foreign policy will be possible.

Education

Education, whether formal or informal, is essential for humans to lead satisfying lives because it allows the realisation of intellectual potential, which is valuable in itself. Self-understanding is contingent on understanding one's social milieu, which in turn requires knowledge of philosophy, ethics and history—precisely the subject areas that have been marginalised by the commodification of education under consumer capitalism. During the last two decades or so education has come increasingly under the influence of market ideology and commercial pressures. The effectiveness of university courses is now measured by the earning potential of graduates, and little importance is attached to the extent to which education can transform students into well-developed human beings who have a deeper understanding of themselves, their societies and the world. Increased public investment in education would be directed at enhancing opportunities to live rich lives rather than attain high incomes.

Poverty and exclusion

For a minority in rich countries, poverty remains entrenched, belying the promise that growth will provide for the poor. Acknowledgment that growth will not solve the problem will

permit a more direct focus on redistributive policies free of soph-
istry and threats of capital strikes. A recasting of tax systems—
including the introduction of luxury taxes, taxes on speculation,
inheritance taxes and ecological taxes, as well as a reinvigoration
of progressive income taxation—would supply the revenue for a
basic income to be provided unconditionally to all citizens. The
provision of a basic income would transform household relations
and contribute to the promotion of the democratic household,
including financial recognition of the benefits of household work
without its commodification.

Environment

Delivered from the fear that protecting the natural world will
damage business confidence, governments would at last be in a
position to take seriously the principles of ecological sustainability. Ecodesign principles should be required in everything,
from office buildings and business equipment to transport
systems and cars.[9] Ecodesign aims to eliminate pollution by
ensuring that firms make ecologically suitable choices in terms
of materials, manufacturing methods and construction processes;
it also aims to reduce resource use to a minimum through the
adoption of 'closed-loop' cycles. Firms would be required to take
responsibility for the materials they use and the wastes they
generate, from cradle to grave. Ecodesign and its cousin, industrial ecology, call for a radical rethinking of how we do things at
every level, so that the principles of sustainability are fully
adopted.

The post-growth economy

It will undoubtedly be said that the post-growth society advocated here is economically irresponsible and will bring about collapse. Those who fetishise the economy are ruled by it and would sooner see the mass of people consigned to lives of alienation and discontent than question the god of GDP. Needless to say, in a post-growth society good economic management will still be required, essentially to avoid recessions that reduce well-being by creating unemployment. It is worth remembering, though, that under the present system governments sometimes deliberately encourage recessions, or make them deeper than they need to be, in the belief that the economy needs a good dose of tonic. One of the advantages of going beyond growth is that governments will no longer be attracted to such aggressive economic management, with its all-too-prevalent mistakes that invariably punish the most vulnerable.

The post-growth society proposed here has much in common with the notion of a stationary state, an idea that can be traced back at least to the time of the classical economists. More recently, interest has been renewed by environmental decline.[10] Although environmentalism is a new phenomenon, stretching back only three decades or so, some of its flavour was anticipated in 19th century debates about the stationary state. John Stuart Mill stressed that a no-growth economy should not be equated with a stagnant society:

> It is scarcely necessary to remark that a stationary condition
> of capital and population implies no stationary state of

human improvement. There would be as much scope as ever for all kinds of mental culture, and moral and social progress; as much room for improving the Art of living, and much more likelihood of its being improved, when minds ceased to be engrossed by the art of getting on.[11]

In an era when almost the entire surface of Earth is managed for the benefit of humans, and the growth of population and consumption pressures show no sign of abating, the stationary state's appeal to the thoughtful observer becomes ever greater. In the rich countries of the West the material consequences of growth are unavoidable: cities become ever more crowded, congestion runs up against the need to do everything more quickly, and more and more land is paved over for housing and roads. In an overcrowded world, it is increasingly difficult to find the solitude needed to sustain the inner self. Mill could barely have imagined such a future:

> If the earth must lose that great portion of its pleasantness which it owes to things that the unlimited increase of wealth and population would extirpate from it, for the mere purpose of enabling it to support a larger, but not a better or happier population, I sincerely hope, for the sake of posterity, that they will be content to be stationary, long before necessity compels them to it.[12]

In 1930 Keynes reflected on what life would be like after another century of economic growth. He anticipated that, with average real incomes perhaps eight times higher, the economic problem would have been well and truly solved. This is the point that has been surpassed by the great majority of people in the West today. In this state, Keynes observed:

> ... for the first time since his creation man will be faced with his real, his permanent problem—how to use his freedom from pressing economic cares, how to occupy the leisure, which science and compound interest will have won for him, to live wisely and agreeably and well ... [I]t will be those people, who can keep alive, and cultivate into a fuller perfection, the art of life itself and do not sell themselves for the means of life, who will be able to enjoy the abundance when it comes.[13]

Despite the abundance provided by sustained growth, few people today keep alive and cultivate the 'art of living' that both Mill and Keynes refer to, and most cannot enjoy the abundance that has arrived. This is the tragedy of consumer capitalism.

In some respects, the post-growth society advocated here is in the same spirit as Mill's stationary state. The argument here is that we should go beyond growth and focus our personal attention and public policies on those aspects of life that do in fact contribute to our wellbeing. Growth can be put to one side. Such a change would mean that working life, the natural environment and the public sector would no longer be sacrificed in order to push up the rate of growth. This would almost certainly mean that the rate of economic growth as it is now measured would decline and may, in time, become negative.

Now let us consider the four main objections that are raised against the stationary state and that will be raised against the post-growth society proposed here. The first is that without growth capitalism will collapse and everything will be thrown into chaos. The most trenchant opponents of capitalism join with its most ardent supporters in this view. The argument from the left derives from Marx's analysis of the accumulation of capital, in which continuing expansion is at the very core of 'the logic of the system'. Neoliberals share this belief in the logic of the system but, like their counterparts on the Left, have difficulty going beyond the mere assertion that capitalism must continue to grow or die. This is not the place to go into a detailed exegesis and critique of the accumulation thesis, but a couple of observations suggest a response. First, if capitalism must continue to grow, must it grow at 4 per cent per annum or will 2 per cent be enough? Would 1 per cent do, or something less? At what point would capitalism collapse? It is common for countries going through the industrialisation process to sustain growth rates of 6 or 8 per cent for two or three decades but then see the rate fall to the 2 or 3 per cent that typifies rich countries. In the 1990s the Japanese economy went through an extended recession in which the average growth rate in the decade to 2002 was around 1 per cent. In a country that had been the envy of the Western world and the model for the Asian tigers, growth effectively stopped for a decade. This has led to much soul-searching and dire predictions of Japan's terminal decline. The country had become habituated to high growth rates, the hook on which national pride was hung. Yet after some years neither the economy nor the society had imploded. Indeed, prominent Japanese economists and commentators began to argue that a zero-growth economy is to be welcomed.[14] They note that, while official unemployment has grown to 5 per cent,[15] the slump has provided an opportunity to change entrenched work practices that have been literally killing people and to trigger a cultural renaissance that might rescue Japan from the emptiness of its affluence. Economic stagnation has provided the opportunity for Japanese society to slow down and reconsider the emphasis that the Japanese growth machine has given to expansion at the cost of families, communities and the natural environment.

The Japanese case can be used to refute the second objection to zero growth—the belief that the forces of globalisation inevitably impose the logic of expansion on national economies. Despite near-zero growth throughout the 1990s, Japan has continued to be a full participant in the world economy and the world community. Its exports and imports are lower than they would have been with a growth rate of 4 or 5 per cent, but that is not a problem as long as the current account remains roughly in balance over the long term. In short, the case of Japan suggests that zero or near-zero growth over an extended period does not mean economic collapse, isolation from the world economy, social disintegration and cultural decline. Zero growth may indeed prove to be a heaven-sent opportunity for a Japanese cultural and social revival. The iron law of accumulation forgot to account for the limitless adaptability of people and their institutions.

A third and more substantial argument against a post-growth society is that unless the growth rate is maximised unemployment will increase and become chronic. There is no doubt that unemployment in our societies causes a great deal of misery, but we must question whether maximising the growth rate is the only or the best way to deal with it. In economics, the informal relationship known as 'Okun's law' suggests that the rate of unemployment will fall by 1 per cent if the real economic growth rate reaches 2.5 per cent above the underlying trend. If we embrace slower growth rates, and eventually perhaps a stationary state, is this not a recipe for mass unemployment? The relationship between growth of the economy and growth of employment is more complicated that Okun's law allows and depends very much on how the question is framed. After all, in the 1950s and 1960s it was widely believed that economic growth would in the foreseeable future relieve us of the need to work. The nature of the growth process and the legal, political and cultural institutions in which growth occurs have a strong bearing on the number and nature of jobs created. Moreover, since the 1970s in Europe chronic unemployment has often seemed intractable even in the presence of strong growth over many years, a situation sometimes referred to as 'jobless growth'. In other words, the relationship between economic growth and employment growth is highly conditional. Certainly, there is no 'desire' on the part of capitalism to create jobs and resolve unemployment, so that job growth is an accident of the system. Indeed, it is often the case that the financial markets react poorly to a reduction in unemployment, sparking a sell-off that helps dampen the economy and shed jobs.

In the longer term, stabilising population size will reduce the pressure to create new jobs each year so as to absorb new entrants to the labour market. Of course, the principal characteristic of a post-growth society is that people no longer feel the compulsion to consume as much, and as a result most will need to devote less time to paid employment. In other words, while a lower growth rate would reduce the demand for labour, falling interest in consumption would mean less labour supplied to the market. This provides the right environment for policies aimed at redistributing work from those who have too much to those who have too little. Such policies are already being introduced in some countries. In 1998 the French government legislated for a 35-hour week, to apply from the beginning of 2000, with no loss of pay and with penalties for employers who fail to comply. Significant numbers of citizens of rich countries have already decided to accept lower levels of material consumption, and many more would like to make such a change if the conditions were more conducive. Moreover, the level of employment depends heavily on choices that are made about the mix of capital, resources and labour used in production processes. In a post-growth society— in which sustainability is taken seriously—a suite of policies, including ecological tax reform, would encourage substitution of labour for natural resource use and, less so, capital.

A fourth objection to the post-growth society is the belief that without the preoccupation with making money the incentives that motivate humans to achieve will evaporate and we will be left with a society of lazy lotus-eaters—except that no one will bother tending the lotuses. There is little evidence to sustain this belief, and it is more plausible to believe that humans are predisposed to engage in purposeful activity. After all, one of the most corrosive effects of unemployment is the lethargy it generates in some people, and one of the keys to 'successful ageing' is to remain active. Nor should we fall for the hoary argument that capitalism is the inevitable expression of the selfishness and greed of 'human nature'. Selfishness and greed are socially conditioned (and, as it happens, make their bearers miserable). The apologists of market capitalism, including conventional economists, have simply annexed 'human nature' for their own purposes. But even Adam Smith, to whom the neoliberals improperly trace their belief that the systematic pursuit of self-interest is the best way to advance society's interest, had a more subtle and complete understanding of human motivation. Already in society today there are large numbers of people who have decided to devote themselves to activities other than market-based ones aimed at more income and consumption, even though they might be richer doing otherwise. Artists come to mind, as do the armies of talented people who work for third-sector organisations such as the Red Cross and Greenpeace, not to mention the huge numbers of self-employed people who choose to accept lower incomes in order to have a degree of autonomy and flexibility in their working arrangements. These people are the forerunners of the post-growth society.

There is no doubt that in a post-growth society the nature of the economy and economic activity will change markedly with time, so that growth as conventionally defined will lose much of its relevance. But let us consider what might happen to the 'old economy' in the years of transition. It may well be the case that the economy, as traditionally understood and measured, continues to grow at an annual rate of perhaps 1 or 2 per cent, instead of the 3 or 4 per cent that characterises advanced economies in 'good' years. In the longer term, as people turn their efforts to the activities that really do contribute to improved well-being and happier communities, the growth of output in the market economy will slow and perhaps even decline. If a society was serious about pursuing wellbeing, a contraction of the old economy should not be a concern. The emphasis given to market-based activity will decline as people direct some of their energies elsewhere, so that the amount of paid work (the particular activities that GDP measures) might decline. On the other hand, other productive activities will increase, including those in the household sector, self-improving activities such as education, creative pursuits, and a range of voluntary activities in the community. GDP will fall, but an indicator of national progress that more comprehensively measured productive activity would show continued growth.

With time, a post-growth society will undoubtedly witness far-reaching changes in the structure of the market economy. For instance, restrictions on manipulative marketing would see the vast resources of the advertising industry redirected to more worthwhile and creative pursuits. Many economic activities that are essentially parasitic and make no contribution to social welfare, other than the incomes they provide to the corporations in question, will slowly wither away. Large segments of the financial services industry, especially those involved in speculation and tax avoidance, will no longer be supported. And, as people increasingly understand the false promise of consumption, industries devoted to producing luxury goods—which represent perhaps a quarter of the modern economy—will decline.

What about the empires built by industrialists and entrepreneurs driven by the desire to accumulate fortunes? Society will no longer worship at their feet or be persuaded to sacrifice social justice and the environment on the altar of corporate profit. Nor does human inventiveness have to wither as growth slows. Economic growth has merely channelled much of human inventiveness into commercial ends. Technology has been of incalculable benefit to humanity, yet there is no reason to believe that investment in new technology will collapse in a post-growth society. It is erroneous to believe that humans become creative only in response to financial incentives. Humans will remain as creative and inquiring as ever, and technological developments will continue. Indeed, they may even accelerate, especially those devoted to environment protection and remediation. The nature of technological development will, however, change. Corporations driven solely by the profit motive will no longer determine the direction of technological development: more technological development will be motivated by its own logic and an antici- pated social benefit. Indeed, huge amounts of resources are today directed into technological developments and creative pursuits that are completely trivial and make no contribution to human wellbeing. Corporations employ hordes of highly trained special- ists to develop ways of frivolously differentiating their products from those of their competitors, so that the degree of choice between products is so extensive that consumers find decision making difficult. They then employ hordes of creative people whose task is to market these goods, with the objective of creating the impression that trifling differences in products will make a large difference to the consumer's quality of life.

Power and social structure

Does advocacy of a post-growth society mean we have given up on the poor? The implication of such a question is that societies dominated by the growth fetish can look after the poor, a highly dubious presumption. Nevertheless, it is beyond dispute that in the last century or so in the industrialised North sustained growth has raised the greater part of society out of poverty and delivered a level of affluence that once ordinary folk could only dream about. For all its drawbacks, the process of development, or industrialisation, has proved over time that it can greatly improve the general standard of living, even if it does tend to serve the interests of elites. The question we must confront is whether, once a country has reached an advanced state of development, further growth will eradicate residual poverty. The historical record is not encouraging. In the last 30 years average real incomes in most rich countries have at least doubled, yet poverty remains as entrenched as ever. Generalising across disparate OECD countries, perhaps around 10 per cent of households fit any reasonable definition of poverty and perhaps another 5–10 per cent are having difficulty making ends meet. Of the rest, perhaps half would declare that they are struggling—and not just the bottom half—but few would be able to look the average Bangladeshi in the eye and complain about their financial situation.

Adhering to the Left's 'deprivation model' actually reinforces the arguments and political position of conservatives and prevents us from tackling poverty. The deprivation model is simply the obverse of the growth model; they are both preoccupied with more income. The money obsession was at the heart of the so-called middle-class tax revolt that was begun by Reagan and has provided the psychological foundation for conservative politics ever since, including attacks on welfare for the poor, the rise of middle-class welfare, tax-cutting competitions, loss of confidence in government, and a general shift towards 'private choice'. We now hear social democratic leaders criticising their conservative opponents for setting taxes too high. Why? Because they have accepted that they must play on the private selfishness of the middle classes at the expense of public provision of services and decent welfare systems. In other words, growth fetishism—including the Left's deprivation-model variation of it—militates against further efforts to reduce poverty because it reinforces the belief that more income is the solution and that those with more income are morally more deserving.

A society in which no one cared for others would be a type of hell. But this indispensable compassion should not provide the driving force for a politics of social change in a society where the great majority of people are surrounded by abundance rather than deprivation. The reason we have been unable to make the changes to social structures that are needed if we are to reduce residual poverty is the preoccupation of most of the population with protecting their income, a preoccupation reinforced every time a political party declares that its first priority is more growth.

Of course, the circumstances outside the rich countries are quite different. But we must ask ourselves whether the continued preoccupation with growth in the rich countries of the North is in the interests of people in poor countries in the South—who do indeed need growth, although perhaps of a different variety. In the first place, the principal reason that the United States exerts strong political, and sometimes military, influence in developing countries is its desire to protect the commercial interests of US corporations. Corporate interests are given privilege because they are the agents of economic growth, and it is accepted that growth is the most important objective. Second, in developing countries a debate has raged for decades over the 'trickle-down' hypothesis, the idea that economic growth itself will see wealth seep down to those at the bottom and raise them out of poverty. This idea absolves governments of the responsibility to do anything other than promote free-market policies and structures that maximise the rate of economic growth. Whatever the merits of the trickle-down theory in poor countries, it certainly stops working beyond a certain point in rich countries. Sustained policy intervention in rich countries can make a difference, but the spread of growth fetishism has been associated with a growing reluctance on the part of governments, and societies, to make the necessary 'sacrifices'.

Why have levels of foreign aid sunk so low at a time of unprecedented wealth, if not for the fact that the more wealthy we are the more greedy we become? In a society of greedy people, there are few votes in giving to the poor. Yet aid and investment can contribute far more to improving the lot of ordinary people in developing countries than in countries that are already rich. What would happen if governments in the North decided that they would no longer facilitate investment through tax breaks and opening up new resources for development? What would happen if governments in the North encouraged their citizens to work less, earn less and buy less? In all likelihood capital that could find no profitable outlet in wealthy countries would go to the poorer countries of the South, where, given the right controls, it could do much more to raise the standard of human wellbeing. Moreover, once they had overcome their growth fetish, nations of the North would be more inclined to accept the arguments of the South for fair trade, rather than succumb to the demands of Northern corporations for unfettered access to the South's markets, public assets, intellectual property and genetic resources.

The growth fetish organises the distribution of power in society today, so relegation of growth to the second order of public and private priorities would inevitably carry with it a restructuring of power. The result would be a more egalitarian society, achieved not so much by redistribution of income but by depriving the wealthy of much of the power and status that attaches to their wealth. In a democratic polity, the exercise of power by those who control capital depends above all on society acceding to the belief that more wealth is essential to greater happiness, for it is this belief that accords capital the pivotal role in social advancement. The structure of society and the practice of government are then framed around the so-called creators of wealth, since they are seen as the creators of happiness. But in a post-growth society class division based on differences in wealth and the ability to generate wealth will melt away. In this sense, the post-growth society will for the first time create the possibility of a classless society.

In classical Marxist analysis, class divisions are based primarily on the concentration of ownership of capital, so that most people, dispossessed of the ability to provide for themselves independently, can survive only by selling their labour to the owners of capital. In so doing, they sacrifice their independence because their labour power, their life force, becomes the property of another. The distinction between capitalists and proletarians mattered because of what it meant for the distribution of power. The objective economic and political circumstances that gave rise to this situation have changed radically since the 19th century, and especially in the last 50 years, yet our social structures, values and political systems continue to be rooted in the old model, in which the choice for most was selling one's labour or starving to death.

How have the objective circumstances changed to render the old model redundant? Because of technological and organisational advance we are vastly wealthier, so that survival through working long hours is no longer the only option. A large proportion of the labour force can choose to work more or less. Only about half the workforce are now non-managerial employees of private firms. The rest are managers, self-employed workers, or employees of the public sector. Substantial numbers of people have increased their 'bargaining power' by working at jobs that give them more personal control, even if it means a lower income. So, for a significant proportion of the workforce in Western society, the chains of wage labour have fallen away.

A society that refused to accept the belief that accumulation of wealth is the source of national progress would rob capital of much of its power. Whereas Marxism called for the power of capital to be destroyed, eudemonism calls for it to be ignored. This possibility is permitted by the presence of abundance and democracy. The space left by the decline in the influence of business will be filled by those who can facilitate the changes that do contribute to a better society and happier people. Governments will begin to act more directly for the community. The voices of community groups arguing for social justice, environment protection and liberation will become the mainstream. Social justice and environment protection will no longer be pursued only to the extent that they do not hinder growth; they will be pursued for their contribution to national and community wellbeing.

By elevating economic growth to their first priority and adapting the provision of public services to neoliberal principles, governments have become inextricably committed to reinforcing the belief systems and social structures that sustain the growth fetish and consumer capitalism. Government, as the expression of collective interests, must be renewed so that its role is to advance national wellbeing by providing an environment in which individuals and social groups can pursue authentic ways of achieving fulfilment and recognition. The primary function of government in a post-growth society will be to protect, expand and enrich our social, cultural and natural capital. Undoubtedly, the transition to such a society will meet enormous resistance from within the structures of governance. At present, the growth fetish places finance ministries at the top of the bureaucratic pyramid. Good economic management will continue to be important, but making the 'hard' decisions to ensure a growth rate of 4 per cent instead of 3 per cent will no longer be government's principal objective. This development will be welcomed by the ministries of environment, education and social security, and we could expect the distribution of talent within bureaucracies to become more even.

In time, in a post-growth society the nature of relationships between people will change. At present much of our interaction with others is conditioned by the identities we manufacture from the raw material marketers provide and by judgments about status based on differences in wealth. Pursuit of money, the benchmark by which success is largely judged, is inseparable from a society based on competition. The point is that the means by which people judge their success is something that is in limited supply, so for every winner there must be losers. The personal costs of such a structure are enormous because a competitive society contrives to make the losers feel bad about themselves. In a post-growth society, the measures of achievement will be more diffuse and will tend to focus much more on the development of each person's inner potential, creativity and social contribution. These markers of achievement are not in limited supply—the attainment of more by one person does not diminish the amount available for others—so society will inevitably be less competitive. This is not to say that humans will give up striving: the desire to achieve seems to be hard-wired into humans, or at least its cultural roots are so deep that they are perhaps ineradicable. But striving and achievement can take many forms, and the indicators of achievement and worth are socially conditioned.

These are some of the more obvious changes that characterise a post-growth society. There will, however, be more subtle and far-reaching changes. The principal objection of progressive people to the current social structure is that it is unequal. This is not just a preoccupation of the political Left: surveys in rich countries consistently confirm that a large majority of people believe that the distribution of wealth is unfair. As we have seen, many studies show that people judge the adequacy of their incomes less by their absolute levels and more by comparison with others. The result is that when everyone's income rises, most are left feeling worse off. Some people come to understand that the difference between feeling worse off and feeling better off is a simple change of attitude that anyone can adopt at any time. Yet people are subjected daily to a fusillade of messages that make them feel dissatisfied, even though they are objectively more wealthy.

Instead of higher incomes, the central objective of a post-growth society is to provide opportunities for human fulfilment and self-realisation. Pursuit of wellbeing—which for many will require abandonment of the money obsession and rejection of the pursuit of identity through consumption—would allow the emergence of authentic (rather than manufactured) individuality and the flowering of human potential. This potential has many forms and will bring many surprises, but it will offer greater opportunity for intellectual and cultural growth and the ability to understand ourselves as we evolve through life. It will allow us to begin to understand what is actually worthwhile and fulfilling, as opposed to what advertisers and the marketing society tell us will give us meaningful lives.

Two years after the fall of white rule, I visited South Africa to help set up a policy research centre. A black South African who had spent years in the struggle against apartheid told me that he and his comrades had always feared the white government and system of apartheid as an enormously powerful and nigh-unbeatable force that spread oppression across the land. As the regime began to crumble in the early 1990s, leading to a multi-racial transitional government in 1993, he began to see the apartheid regime as more like *The Wizard of Oz*. When Dorothy first meets the Wizard she quakes before a towering dark figure with a booming voice. But after a time she peeks behind a curtain to see a frail old man pedalling a machine that creates the illusion of a huge and terri-fying wizard. Nothing is inevitable and no power is invincible.

Notes

Chapter 1   Growth fetishism

1   This phrase is from Marx's discussion of commodity fetishism, in Robert Tucker, *The Marx–Engels Reader*, W.W. Norton and Company, New York, 1972, p. 215.

2   Gavan McCormack, *The Emptiness of Japanese Affluence*, M.E. Sharpe, Armonk, NY, 1996, pp. 289–90.

3   John Stuart Mill, *Principles of Political Economy, with Some of Their Applications to Social Philosophy*, 6th edn, Longmans, Green and Co., London, 1923, p. 746. Mill's *Principles* was first published in 1848; the sixth edition was first published in 1865.

4   ibid., pp. 748–9. In the first edition, Mill noted that America (except in the South) had attained an advanced state of wealth and political freedoms but, he observed sardonically, 'All that these advantages seem to have done for them is that the life of the whole of one sex is devoted to dollar-hunting, and of the other to breeding dollar-hunters' (p. 748, note 1).

5   E.J. Mishan, *The Costs of Economic Growth*, Staples Press, London, 1967, pp. xviii, xix. Anticipating the extraordinary mathematisation of economics in the 1970s and 1980s, Mishan also wrote of the 'mass flight from reality into statistics' (p. 8). This preoccupation with the measurable in economics has been characterised as 'physics envy'.

6   N. Gregory Mankiw, *Principles of Economics*, The Dryden Press, Orlando FL, 1998, p. 489.

7   ibid., p. 489.

8   Quoted by C. Cobb, T. Halstead and J. Rowe, *The Atlantic Monthly*, October 1995.

9   ibid.

10 The Harwood Group, *Yearning for Balance: views of Americans on consumption, materialism, and the environment*, prepared for the Merck Family Fund <www.iisd.ca/linkages/consume/harwood.html>.

11 ibid.

12 Noam Chomsky has, however, argued that the fall of the Berlin Wall was a small victory for socialism.

13 *Sydney Morning Herald*, 29–31 March 2002.

14 Francis Fukuyama, *The End of History and the Last Man*, The Free Press, New York, 1992, pp. xi–xii.

Chapter 2   Growth and wellbeing

1   Steve Dodds, 'Economic growth and human well-being', in Mark Diesendorf and Clive Hamilton (eds), *Human Ecology, Human Economy: ideas towards an ecologically sustainable future*, Allen & Unwin, Sydney, 1997.

2   The rank correlation coefficient between appreciation of life and GDP per capita is 0.71 and the ordinary correlation coefficient is also 0.71.

3   The conclusions based on this table are confirmed by Bruno Frey and Alois Stutzer in *Happiness and Economics*, Princeton University Press, Princeton and Oxford, 2002, Table 2.2.

4   ibid., Figure 1.4 and pp. 74–6.

5   The rank correlation coefficient is 0.71 and the ordinary correlation coefficient is 0.46.

6   A. Wearing and B. Headey, 'Who enjoys life and why? Measuring subjective well-being', in Richard Eckersley (ed.), *Measuring Progress: is life getting better?* CSIRO Publishing, Collingwood, Victoria, 1998.

7   Michael Argyle, 'Sources of satisfaction', in Ian Christie and Lindsay Nash (eds), *The Good Life*, Demos Collection 14, London, 1998, p. 34.

8   See Dodds, 'Economic growth and human well-being', p. 114.

9   Quoted by Dodds, 'Economic growth and human well-being', 1997.

10   Argyle, 'Sources of satisfaction'.

11   Argyle, 'Sources of satisfaction', reviews some of it.

12   Frey and Stutzer, *Happiness and Economics*, p. 83.

13   David Myers, 'Does economic growth improve human morale?', Center for a New American Dream <www.newdream.org> 1997.

14   Ed Diener, Jeff Horwitz and Robert Emmons 1985, 'Happiness of the very wealthy', *Social Indicators Research*, vol. 16, pp. 263–74.

15   Myers, 'Does economic growth improve human morale?'.

16   Frey and Stutzer, *Happiness and Economics*, pp. 9–10.

17   See D.G. Myers and E. Diener, 'The pursuit of happiness', *Scientific American*, no. 274, May, 1996, pp. 54–6.

18   Myers, 'Does economic growth improve human morale?'. See also Frey and Stutzer, *Happiness and Economics*, pp. 76–7.

19   Juliet Schor, *The Overspent American*, HarperCollins, New York, 1999, p. 6.

20   C. Hamilton, *Overconsumption in Australia*, Discussion Paper no. 49, The Australia Institute, Canberra, 2002.

21   Ian Castles, 'Living standards in Sydney and Japanese cities—a comparison', in Kyoko Sheridan (ed.), *The Australian Economy in the Japanese Mirror*, University of Queensland Press, Brisbane, 1992.

22   These figures are for 1987 and may have changed since then, especially the split between males and females.

23   Myers and Diener, 'The pursuit of happiness'.

24 See the paper by Michael Pusey, 'Incomes, standards of living and quality of life', in Eckersley, *Measuring Progress*.

25 Philip Brickman and Dan Coates, 'Lottery winners and accident victims: is happiness relative?', *Journal of Personality and Social Psychology*, vol. 36, no. 8, 1978, pp. 917–27.

26 Myers ('Does economic growth improve human morale?') also makes the nice point that the need to build more storage space in our homes—built-in wardrobes, pantries, extra linen cupboards, kitchens with deep drawers, rumpus rooms, double garages, extra sheds—does not arise from a lack of planning by architects of earlier eras. They built houses that had enough storage space for the times, but nowhere near enough for the vast increase in the volume of goods a typical house must now accommodate. Fewer people, more possessions.

27 Headey and Wearing, quoted by Eckersley, *Measuring Progress*.

28 Robert Emmons, Chi Cheung and Keivan Tehrani, 'Assessing spirituality through personal goals: implications for research on religion and subjective well-being', *Social Indicators Research*, vol. 45, 1998, pp. 391, 393.

29 This section draws on a number of papers: T. Kasser and R. Ryan, 'A Dark Side of the American Dream: correlates of financial success as a central life aspiration', *Journal of Personality and Social Psychology*, vol. 63, 1993, pp. 410–22; T. Kasser and R. Ryan, 'Further examining the American dream: differential correlates of intrinsic and extrinsic goals', *Personality and Social Psychology Bulletin*, vol. 22, 1996, pp. 280–7; T. Kasser and R. Ryan, 'Be careful what you wish for: optimal functioning and the relative attainment of intrinsic and extrinsic goals', in P. Schmuck and K. Sheldon (eds), *Life Goals and Well-being*, Hogrefe & Huber Publishers, Gottingen, 2001; T. Kasser, 'Two versions of the American dream: which goals and values make for a high quality life?' in E. Diener and D. Rahtz (eds), *Advances in Quality of Life Theory and Research*, vol.1, Kluwer, Dordrecht, Netherlands 2000; K. Sheldon and T. Kasser, 'Pursuing personal goals: skills enable progress, but not all progress is beneficial', *Personality and Social Psychology Bulletin*, vol. 24, 1998, pp. 1319–31.

30 Kasser and Ryan, 'Be careful what you wish for'.

31 ibid.

32 ibid. In an interesting twist, the results showed that people who report higher levels of the intrinsic goal of community feeling had higher levels of illicit drug use, a result perhaps explained by the communal use of certain types of drugs.

33 Kasser and Ryan, 'Further examining the American dream', p. 286.

34 Martin Seligman, referred to in Myers, 'Does economic growth improve human morale?', p. 5.

35 Gerald Klerman and Myrna Weissman, 'Increasing rates of depression', *Journal of the American Medical Association*, vol. 261, no. 15, 1989, pp. 229–34.

36 Christopher Murray and Alan Lopez (eds), *The Global Burden of Disease: summary*, Harvard School of Public Health, for WHO and World Bank, Geneva, 1996, p. 21.

37 See Lawrence Diller's website <www.docdiller.com>.

38 Headey and Wearing, quoted by Eckersley, *Measuring Progress*.

39 Carol Ryff, 'Happiness is everything, or is it? Explorations on the meaning of psychological well-being', *Journal of Personality and Social Psychology*, vol. 57, no. 6, 1989, pp. 1069–81.

40 ibid.

41 Emmons et al., 'Assessing spirituality through personal goals', 1998, p. 404.

42 ibid., p. 405.

43 Robert C. Tucker (ed.), *The Marx–Engels Reader*, W.W. Norton & Co., New York, 1972, p. 337.

44 Norman Brown, *Life against Death*, Wesleyan University Press, Connecticut, 1959, p. 251.

45 See, for example, H. Diefenbacher, 'The Index of Sustainable Economic Welfare in Germany', in C. Cobb and J. Cobb (eds), *The Green National Product*, University of Americas Press, 1994; Clive Hamilton, 'The Genuine Progress Indicator: methodological developments and results from Australia', *Ecological Economics*, vol. 30, 1999, pp. 13–28; T. Jackson, N. Marks, J. Ralls and S. Stymne, 'An index of sustainable economic welfare for the UK 1950–1996', Centre for Environmental Strategy, University of Surrey, Guildford, 1997.

46 The factors vary somewhat from country to country, since some are important in some countries but not in others.
47 Although the tide of neoliberalism seems to have made gross inequality more acceptable, particularly in the United States.

Chapter 3   Identity

1 'Only as given wants remain constant and productive activity serves to narrow the margin of discontent between appetites and their gratifications are we justified in talking of an increase in welfare.' E.J. Mishan, *The Costs of Economic Growth*, Staples Press, London, 1967, p. 112.
2 Even here wider society acknowledges that people may be misled into acting against their own interests. Damages awarded to smokers against tobacco companies are a case in point. The use of tobacco appears to be a special case because the damage to health is so direct, incontrovertible and severe. As with most other consumer goods, tobacco advertising promises a range of positive emotional associations—sophistication, coolness, a sense of fun and even, in the more innocent 1950s and 1960s, greater sporting prowess. In contrast with most other consumer goods, tobacco actually delivers (to the addicted smoker) an enormous amount of physical pleasure.
3 It is well established in the retail industry that only 20 per cent of supermarket shoppers are price-sensitive. Another 30 per cent are somewhat influenced by price but it is not the vital factor, while 50 per cent do not take any notice of the price when making purchasing decisions. This fact invalidates the most basic conceptual tool of neoliberal economic theory, the demand curve.
4 M. Csikszentmihalyi and E. Rochberg-Halton, *The Meaning of Things: domestic symbols and the self*, Cambridge University Press, Cambridge, UK, 1981, p. 164.
5 A. Rindfleisch, J. Burroughs and F. Denton, 'Family structure, materialism, and compulsive consumption', *Journal of Consumer Research*, vol. 23, March, 1997.

6   Csikszentmihalyi and Rochberg-Halton, *The Meaning of Things*, p. 229.

7   ibid., p. 230.

8   Quoted by Juliet Schor, *The Overspent American*, Basic Books, New York, 1998, p. 57.

9   Monica Videnieks, 'How gen-X was sold a Chup', *Weekend Australian*, 3–4 June, 2000.

10 Gavan McCormack, *The Emptiness of Japanese Affluence*, M.E. Sharpe, Armonk, NY, 1996, p. 7.

11 ibid., p. 100.

12 R. Lane, 'Friendship or commodities', in N. Goodwin, F. Ackerman and D. Kiron (eds), *The Consumer Society*, Island Press, Washington DC, 1997, p. 102.

13 PBS TV News, 19 October 2001.

14 Richard Wightman Fox and T.J. Jackson Lears (eds), *The Culture of Consumption: critical essays in American history, 1880–1980*, Pantheon Books, New York, 1983, p. xii.

15 Johann Goethe, *Faust*, Part One, Penguin, Harmondsworth, 1949, p. 146.

16 Mishan, *The Costs of Economic Growth*, p. 175.

17 For a polite critique, see <www.Pipedown.com>, the website of the anti-muzak lobby group.

18 John Stuart Mill, *Principles of Political Economy*, 6th edn, Longmans, Green and Co., London 1923, p. 750.

19 The following paragraphs are based on the article by Daniel Pink, 'Metaphor marketing', *Fast Company*, May, 1998.

20 Naomi Klein, *No Logo*, HarperCollins, London, 2001. This and the following quotations are taken from the more succinct version of the argument by Klein in 'The tyranny of the brand', *New Statesman*, 24 January, 2000.

21 ibid.

22 See, especially, <www.adbusters.org>.

23 Advice by the US Federal Trade Commission to House of Representatives, 14 October 1983.

24 Some of the ideas in this section (including the reference to gluttony and sloth) have been stimulated by an unpublished paper by Neil Burry, an Adelaide physician.

25 Figures are drawn from the US Surgeon General <www. surgeongeneral.gov>.
26 ibid.
27 See 'NAASO responds to recent Harris poll on obesity', Press release, 6 March 2002 <www.naaso.org>.
28 G. Egger and B. Swinburn, 'An "ecological" approach to the obesity pandemic', *British Medical Journal*, vol. 355, 1997, pp. 477–80.
29 Schor, *The Overspent American*, p. 19.

Chapter 4   Progress

1 A. Javary, quoted by Morris Ginsberg, *The Idea of Progress: a re-evaluation*, Methuen & Co., London, 1953, p. 1.
2 Ginsberg, ibid., p. 1.
3 From 'The Eighteenth Brumaire of Louis Bonaparte' in *The Marx–Engels Reader*, Robert C. Tucker (ed.), W.W. Norton & Company, New York, 1972, p. 437.
4 Quoted by Ginsberg, *The Idea of Progress*, p. 11.
5 Francis Fukuyama, *The End of History and the Last Man*, The Free Press, New York, 1992, p. xi.
6 ibid., p. xii.
7 ibid., p. xii.
8 ibid., p. xiv.
9 Ulrich Beck, *Democracy without Enemies*, Polity Press, Cambridge, UK, 1998, p. 7.
10 A question posed by Beck, ibid., p. 39.
11 ibid., p. 3.
12 Andre Gorz, *Capitalism, Socialism, Ecology*, trans. Chris Turner, Verso, London, 1994, p. 21.
13 From 'The Communist Manifesto' in *The Marx–Engels Reader*, Robert C. Tucker (ed.), W.W. Norton & Company, New York, 1972, p. 338.
14 The term is from David Brooks, *Bobos in Paradise: the new upper class and how they got there*, Simon & Schuster, New York, 2000.

15   R. Lesthaeghe and G. Moors, 'Recent trends in fertility and household formation in the industrialized world', *Review of Population and Social Policy*, no. 9, 2000, pp. 121–70.

16   Germaine Greer, *The Whole Woman*, Doubleday, London, 1999, pp. 1–2.

17   ibid., p. 309.

18   ibid., pp. 320–1.

19   Introduction to Chris Sheil (ed.), *Globalisation: Australian impacts*, University of New South Wales Press, Sydney, 2001.

20   David Held, Anthony McGrew, David Goldblatt and Jonathan Perraton, *Global Transformations: politics, economics and culture*, Polity Press, Cambridge, UK, 1999.

21   An argument first put forward, with astounding effect, by Lynn White Jr in 'The historical roots of our ecological crisis' in *Science* magazine in 1967. These issues are discussed at more length in Chapter 7.

Chapter 5   Politics

1   Ian Hargreaves and Ian Christie (eds), *Tomorrow's Politics: the Third Way and beyond*, Demos Foundation, London, 1998, p. 1.

2   This definition comes from the 'New Democrats' Progressive Policy Institute <www.ppionline.org>.

3   Anthony Giddens, *The Third Way: the renewal of social democracy*, Polity Press, Cambridge, UK, 1998, p. 2.

4   Giddens, *The Third Way*, p. 69.

5   See the illuminating discussion in Peter Holbrook, 'Left of centre minus the philosophy', *Australian Financial Review*, 18 August 2000.

6   Giddens, *The Third Way*, p. 44.

7   For an analysis of one aspect of this complex question, see Juliet Schor, *The Overspent American*, Basic Books, New York, 1998.

8   The terms derive, respectively, from Robert Reich, *The Work of Nations* (Alfred A. Knopf, New York, 1991) and David Brooks, *Bobos in Paradise* (Simon & Schuster, New York, 2000).

9   A fantasy of the Australian Third Way politician Mark Latham in 'Marxism, social-ism, and the Third Way', *Arena Magazine*, vol. 42, August–September, 1999.

10 Geoffrey Wheatcroft, 'Monica's year', *Prospect*, January, 1999.

11 *The Times* (London), 10 June, 2002.

12 Giddens, *The Third Way*, p. 2.

13 ibid., p. 26.

14 For a sharp, popular critique see James Galbraith, 'How the economists got it wrong', *The American Prospect*, vol. 11, no. 7, 2000.

15 David Card and Alan Krueger, *Myth and Measurement: the new economics of the minimum wage*, Princeton University Press, Princeton, 1997.

16 Joseph Stiglitz, 'What I learned at the world economic crisis', *The New Republic*, 17 April, 2000.

17 A. Fishlow, C. Gwin, S. Haggard and D. Rodrik, *Miracle or Design? Lessons From the East Asian Experience*, Overseas Development Council, Washington, DC, 1994.

18 Giddens, *The Third Way*, p. 40.

19 ibid., p. 109.

20 Latham, 'Marxism, social-ism, and the Third Way'.

21 'Unambiguously' may be too strong a word. After all, some members of Christian religious orders willingly commit themselves to poverty, as do some sufis, monks and saddhus from Eastern spiritual traditions.

Chapter 6   Work

1   The distinction between liberation of and from work is made in Andre Gorz, *Capitalism, Socialism, Ecology*, trans. Chris Turner, Verso, London, 1994, p. 54.

2   As noted in Chapter 5, the terms come, respectively, from Robert Reich (*The Work of Nations*, Alfred A. Knopf, New York, 1991) and David Brooks (*Bobos in Paradise*, Simon & Schuster, 2000).

3   Craig Thompson and Siok Kuan Tambyah, 'Trying to be cosmopolitan', *Journal of Consumer Research*, December, 1999.

4   Quoted by Gorz, *Capitalism, Socialism, Ecology*, p. 59.

5   ibid., p. 61.

6   This raises an awkward question: If work is alienating, but is essential to sustain high levels of consumption, what happens when consumption is alienating too?

7   See John Haworth, *Work, Leisure and Well-being*, Routledge, London, 1997, pp. 24–5.

8   Quoted by Haworth, ibid., pp. 25–6.

9   Some cases are discussed by Richard Sennett in his book *The Corrosion of Character*, W.W. Norton, New York, 1998.

10 Haworth, *Work, Leisure and Well-being*, p. 31.

11 *Fortune*, 19 September 1994.

12 Gavan McCormack, *The Emptiness of Japanese Affluence*, M.E. Sharpe, Armonk, NY, 1996, p. 80. The extent to which hours in Japan exceed those in other countries, and indeed the whole question of which countries have the longest hours, is debated.

13 ibid., pp. 82, 85.

14 Gorz, *Capitalism, Socialism, Ecology*, p. 73.

15 Harald Bielenski, Gerhard Bosch and Alexandra Wagner, *Working Time Preferences in Sixteen European Countries*, European Foundation for the Improvement of Living and Working Conditions, Dublin, 2002, Table 16.

16 ibid.

17 John Maynard Keynes, 'Economic possibilities for our grandchildren', *Essay In Persuasion*, W.W. Norton & Co., New York, 1963, p. 361.

18 ibid.

19 Bielenski, *Working Time Preferences*, Figures 6–8.

20 Sennett, *The Corrosion of Character*, p. 23.

21 ibid., p. 25.

22 ibid., p. 26.

23 ibid., pp. 9, 120.

24 Sennett (ibid., p. 122) makes this distinction.
25 For Canada see M. Anielski and J. Rowe, *The Genuine Progress Indicator: 1998 update*, Redefining Progress, San Francisco, 1999. For Australia, where hours of housework per adult have been very stable, at around 26 per week, see C. Hamilton and R. Denniss, *Tracking Well-being: the Genuine Progress Indicator 2000*, Discussion paper no. 35, The Australia Institute, Canberra, 2000. For the United States see J. Schor, *The Overworked American*, Basic Books, New York, 1991, pp. 86–7.
26 The *Journal of Political Economy*, reproduced in G. Becker, *The Economic Approach to Human Behavior*, University of Chicago Press, Chicago, 1976.
27 Gorz, *Capitalism, Socialism, Ecology*, p. 63.
28 The term is due to James Robertson—*Future Work*, Gower Publishing Co., Aldershot, UK, 1985.
29 Gorz, *Capitalism, Socialism, Ecology*, p. 21.

Chapter 7   Environment

1 World Resources Institute, September 2000 <www.wri.org>.
2 Herman Daly, 'From empty-world to full-world economics', in R. Goodland, H. Daly and S. El Serafy (eds), *Environmentally Sustainable Economic Development: building on Brundtland*, UNESCO, Paris, 1991, p. 30.
3 William Laurence, 'Future shock: forecasting a grim fate for the Earth', *Trends in Ecology and Evolution*, vol. 16, no. 10, 2001.
4 Mathis Wackernagel, 'Tracking the ecological overshoot of the human economy', *Proceedings of the National Academy of Science*, vol. 99, no. 14, 2002.
5 ibid.
6 OECD, *Economic Instruments for Pollution Control and Natural Resource Management in OECD Countries: a survey*, OECD Environment Directorate, Paris, 1999.

7   See, for example, Environmental Defense, *From Obstacle to Opportunity: how acid rain emissions trading is delivering cleaner air*, Environmental Defense, New York, 2000.

8   National Academies of Science, *Abrupt Climate Change: inevitable surprises*, Committee on Abrupt Climate Change, National Research Council, National Academy Press, Washington DC, 2002.

9   See, for example, Intergovernmental Panel on Climate Change, *Climate Change 2001: synthesis report*, Robert Watson (ed.), Cambridge University Press, Cambridge, UK, 2001, p. 343.

10 In fact, a survey commissioned by the Union of Concerned Scientists in July 2002 concluded that 76 per cent of US citizens want their government to require power plants and industry to reduce their greenhouse gas emissions. Despite widespread concern, the issue has not gained enough political traction for people to take to the streets over it.

11 Mathis Wackernagel, *Ecological Footprints of Nations: How much nature do they use? How much nature do they have?* <www.ecouncil.ac.cr/rio/focus/report/english/footprint/>, 1997.

12 Quoted in G. Reynolds, 'Space property rights', *Ad Astra*, September October, 1998.

13 Virtually nothing has been written on the subject. UN treaties dating from the 1950s and 1960s reserve space for the common benefit of humankind. At a seminar in Copenhagen in 2000, Vigdis Finnbogattodir, the former President of Iceland, posed the question, 'Who will take responsibility for outer space?'

14 Warwick Fox's *Towards a Transpersonal Ecology* (Shambhala, Boston, 1990) is an excellent discourse on these questions. The subsequent paragraphs draw heavily on Fox.

15 David Pearce, *Blueprint for a Green Economy*, Earthscan, London, 1989.

16 Fox, *Towards a Transpersonal Ecology*.

17 Interestingly, the Catholic Church appears to have formally accepted such a view. Calling for an 'ecological conversion', in 2001 Pope John Paul II declared that humanity 'is no longer the Creator's "steward", but an autonomous despot, who is finally beginning to understand that [it] must stop at the edge of the

abyss'. He called for a new philosophy that recognises 'the fundamental good of life in all its manifestations', a life-based ethic akin to that advanced by Albert Schweitzer.

18 Quoted in Fox, *Towards a Transpersonal Ecology*, p. 176.

19 In the words of George Sessions, quoted in Fox, *Towards a Transpersonal Ecology*, p. 225.

20 Max Weber, *Economy and Society*, Bedminster Press, New York, 1968, p. 376.

21 Rogers Brubaker, *The Limits to Rationality*, George Allen and Unwin, London, 1984, p. 10.

22 Weber, *Economy and Society*, p. 86.

23 James Poterba, quoted in J. MacKenzie, R. Dower and D. Chen, *The Going Rate: what it really costs to drive*, World Resources Institute <www.wri.org>, 1992.

24 V. Brajer, 'Recent evidence on the distribution of air effects', *Contemporary Policy Issues*, vol. 10, no. 2, 1992, pp. 63–71.

25 John Donovan, *Lead in Children: report on the National Survey of Lead in Children*, Australian Institute of Health and Welfare, Canberra, 1996.

26 World Bank, *Indonesia: growth, infrastructure and human resources*, World Bank, Jakarta, 1992, p. 53.

27 See, for example, David Imber, Gay Stevenson, and Leanne Wilks, *A Contingent Valuation Survey of the Kakadu Conservation Zone*, Resource Assessment Commission research paper no. 3, Australian Government Publishing Service, Canberra, 1991.

Chapter 8   The post-growth society

1 Juliet Schor, *The Overspent American*, HarperCollins, New York, 1999, p. 22.

2 Clive Hamilton and Elizabeth Mail, *Downshifting in Australia: a sea-change in the pursuit of happiness*, Discussion Paper no. 50, The Australia Institute, Canberra, 2003.

3 Juliet Schor, *The Overspent American*, pp. 113–15.

4 Hamilton and Mail, *Downshifting in Australia*, Table 5.
5 The *Oxford English Dictionary* defines 'eudemonism' (also spelt eudæmonism) as the 'system of ethics which finds the moral standard in the tendency of actions to produce happiness', and traces its first use to 1827.
6 Andre Gorz, *Capitalism, Socialism, Ecology*, trans. Chris Turner, Verso, London, 1994, p. 30.
7 ibid., p. 5.
8 Although doing so without commodifying and imposing market rationality on household activities.
9 Janis Birkland, Mark Diesendorf and Clive Hamilton, 'Some pathways to ecological sustainability', in Mark Diesendorf and Clive Hamilton (eds), *Human Ecology, Human Economy*, Allen & Unwin, Sydney, 1997.
10 See especially Herman Daly, 'The economics of the steady state', *American Economic Review*, vol. 64, 1974, pp. 15–21.
11 John Stuart Mill, *Principles of Political Economy, with Some of Their Applications to Social Philosophy*, 6th edn, Longmans, Green and Co., London, 1923, p. 751.
12 ibid., pp. 750–1.
13 John Maynard Keynes, 'Economic possibilities for our grandchildren' in *Essays in Persuasion*, W.W. Norton, New York, 1963, p. 362.
14 Gavan McCormack, 'Demolishing the Doken Kokka? The Japanese struggle to get over the growth obsession', Unpublished paper, Australian National University, Canberra, 2002.
15 McCormack suggests the real figure in 2001 was closer to 10.4 per cent: Gavan McCormack, 'The end of Japan's construction state?', *New Left Review*, vol. 13, Jan–Feb, 2002, p. 2.

Index